THE WASHINGTON D.C. ART REVIEW

A LES KRANTZ BOOK

THE WASHINGTON D.C. ART REVIEW

The Art Explorer's Guide to Washington

By Frank Getlein and
Jo Ann Lewis

Cover Photo By Dennis Kan
Design By Bill Lowry

The Vanguard Press, New York

Published by The Vanguard Press, Inc.
in cooperation with The Krantz Company

Library of Congress Catalogue Number: 80-53-843
ISBN: 0-8149-0832-2

Manufactured in the United States of America

Contents

The reader may find the sales gallery or museum exhibiting any of the listed artists by consulting the appropriate page number. Some galleries and museums exhibit various artists on a one-time basis or as part of rotating exhibits, thus a phone call is recommended for verification.

Foreword

Washington has been known as the American city of museums since early in this century, when the Smithsonian Institution first began to spread its wings, to make of "the nation's attic" a supple and effective instrument of instruction and delight for all Americans visiting their capital. It was not, however, until just before and after World War II that the art museums of Washington began catching up. The first giant step was the joining of the National Gallery of Art to the long-established Corcoran Gallery, Phillips Collection, and Freer Gallery. A more recent explosion of art museums—the National Collection of Fine Arts, the National Portrait Gallery, the Hirshhorn Collection, along with more specialized efforts such as the Textile Museum and the Museum of African Art, has placed the nation's capital in a position of primacy in the museum world.

Similarly, commercial galleries were few or non-existent before World War II. The now-venerable Franz Bader, then a Viennese refugee, began a movement that has now proliferated all over town and out into the suburbs. The movement was assuredly helped by the flowering of the Washington School of Color Painting as one of the chief nominees to succeed Abstract Expressionism.

At any rate, the art of museums and the art of private galleries are now, at long last, thoroughly established in Washington. The following pages celebrate that fact and are testimony to the richness at hand.

The Museums

The Museums

Anacostia

Anacostia Neighborhood Museum 2405 Martin Luther King, Jr., Ave. SE 381-6691 Monday-Friday: 10-6, Saturday and Sunday: 1-6 Admission free

For the visitor interested in museums as such and for black Americans interested in how museums can address black problems, the trip across Washington's other river, the Anacostia, and into one of the city's more impoverished areas, is well worth the effort. In the 1960s, the American museum profession was much concerned with the idea of museums as "instruments for social change." The Anacostia Neighborhood Museum is probably the most enduring and in some ways the most revolutionary result of that professional preoccupation. Most neighborhood museums that came into being in those years limited themselves to bringing small samples, as it were, from the "big house" to assorted small houses in areas where residents rarely got into downtown museums. The Anacostia, in contrast, from its founding in 1967, aimed to bring historical and social understanding to the residents of its depressed area through its research and its exhibitions. The museum made its first devastating impact on Washington consciousness with "The Rat," in 1969, not a political biography but a scientific, sociological, medical guide to a permanent feature of life in Anacostia. Since then, exhibitions have explored area history, African themes, the social situation of blacks and particularly black women. The museum is a subsidiary of the Smithsonian Institution, but largely the creation of its founder-director, John R. Kinard. There is no permanent collection, but the special exhibitions are always stimulating, even when they focus on appalling reality.

Corcoran

The Corcoran Gallery of Art 17th St. and New York Ave. NW. 638-3211 Tuesday-Sunday: 11-4:30 Closed Mondays and national holidays Admission free

The Building

The Corcoran Gallery of Art is not only the oldest art museum in Washington, it is one of the three oldest major art museums in the country, along with the Metropolitan in New York and the Boston

Museum of Fine Arts, all of which opened their doors in 1869. The Corcoran was actually established ten years earlier, but before the specially commissioned building was completed the Civil War had started, and the new structure was commandeered for various wartime purposes. It is now the Renwick Gallery (q.v.). The founder was William Wilson Corcoran, a Washington banker who made his fortune selling the government bonds issued to finance the war with Mexico.

The present structure was built by the trustees within a decade of Mr. Corcoran's death. Opening in 1897, it amply demonstrates the grandeur of the Gilded Age associated with high art. It also testifies to the exhilarating pleasure of nonutilitarian space. On the ground floor and on the main floor, the double atrium, complete with classical columns, encourages the mind to open up. Like the grand staircases at the Metropolitan and the Louvre, the Corcoran's staircase conveys the subliminal message that art is an experience to which we ascend. The noble facade is embellished with the names of those considered world-class artists in the 1890s, and the only one most visitors fail to recognize is the single American, Allston. The two lions guarding the steps from the street are bronze replicas of those the neoclassic sculptor Antonio Canova created for St. Paul's Basilica in Rome.

The Collections

The great strength of the Corcoran Gallery has always been the American collection. Thanks to a grant from the National Endowment for the Arts, the American pictures—and a considerably less inclusive collection of American sculpture—are now hung in a permanent arrangement along the south side of the main floor, and in three rooms on the west side of that floor. The visitor can easily and logically proceed from our colonial beginnings through the mid-twentieth century with, reasonably enough, stress on the "Washington School of Color Painters."

The colonial paintings begin with an "unidentified gentleman" painted by an "unidentified painter"—clearly made for each other—but progress rapidly to one of our earliest known American portraitists, John Smibert, in, almost miraculously for that era, a portrait of a pre-Revolutionary colonial still known, at least at second hand, by most Americans: Peter Faneuil, the Boston merchant who gave his city the famous hall that bears his name and is still used for political occasions. Feke, Wollaston, and Matthew Pratt are also represented in colonial portraiture, and the finest of our colonial portraitists, John Singleton Copley, is seen in a portrait of Col. Jacob Fowle, or Fowler, appropriately holding a gun. It is mildly ironic that Col. Fowle(r) served as an officer of the Massachusetts militia and led protests against the British excise taxes, while Copley married the daughter of a rival Boston merchant whose tea was destroyed in the harbor and who fled the country before the Revolution to become a leading British painter in London for the last 40 years of his life.

Another expatriate to London, Benjamin West, first president of the Royal Academy in London, is represented in the neoclassic pictures then fashionable—*Cupid Stung by a Bee, Cupid and Psyche,* and *Telemachus and Calypso*, from the *Odyssey.*

The first generation of the painting Peales is seen in a pair of portraits and in one of the earliest American still lifes, while his nephew, Rembrant Peale, has a group of works in the collection, including the equestrian portrait of *Washington Before Yorktown* and one of Lt. Col. Joseph Bogart, who invented artillery in America for the War of 1812. There are numerous other portraits, but one of the great treasures of the Corcoran is *The Old House of Representatives* by Samuel F. B. Morse, a founder and first president of the National Academy of Design and later inventor of the telegraph. The *House* painting is extraordinary in several ways, including the handling of space and light and the fact that it contains 86 individual portraits, all identified.

In one sense, American painting really came into its own with the discovery of landscape as a subject. The Corcoran landscapes begin with those of Thomas Cole, founder of the Hudson River School. Interestingly, in addition to the turbulent *Tornado*, a typical Cole dramatization of landscape at its best, the Corcoran has two matched pre-landscape Coles, *The Departure* and *The Return,* apparently based on the romances of Walter Scott. An unusually energetic seascape by Fitz Hugh Lane, complete with a square-rigger about to crash into the easel and an Asher Durand forest scene are highlights of American landscape painting in the earlier nineteenth century.

Genre painting, the other side of the coin of American nineteenth-century art is well represented in William Sidney Mount's *The Long Story* and Richard Caton Woodville's *Waiting for the Stage.*

The West, which was an enduring part of the American dream throughout the nineteenth century, is portrayed in many aspects, reaching peaks, so to speak in *Crossing the Rockies* by Brewton, and in scenes by Bingham and, a great favorite at the Corcoran, Bierstadt. Later nineteenth-century landscape artists include Worthington Whittredge, Sanford Gifford, Jasper Cropsey, George Inness, and Frederick Church, who is present in one of his most famous pictures, *Niagara Falls,* complete with rainbow. Three great American masterpieces by expatriate artists are in the Corcoran collection: Whistler's *Battersea Reach,* Sargent's *Oyster Gatherers of Cancale,* and Mary Cassatt's *Woman With a Dog.* The nineteenth-century giants who stayed home are no less strongly represented: Eakins, Homer and Ryder, Blakelock, Duveneck, and William Merritt Chase.

At about this point in the Corcoran's sweeping survey of American painting there is a small gallery containing half a dozen or so pictures of feminine interiors around the turn of the century, by Tarbell Metcalf, Melchers, Dewing, and others. Nothing quite like it exists in any other museum, and it well repays a little contemplation and meditation from the point of view of both art and history—an American Intimism—and Women's Lib: the women are sewing, talking to a friend, reading or writing a letter, simply sitting, but they are themselves, neither objects of adulation nor adjuncts to rich husbands.

The Eight, the Ash Can School, perpetuates the joy its members found in the artist's life in the Corcoran collection: a portrait of John Sloan by Robert Henri shows the best known of the group looking remarkably like

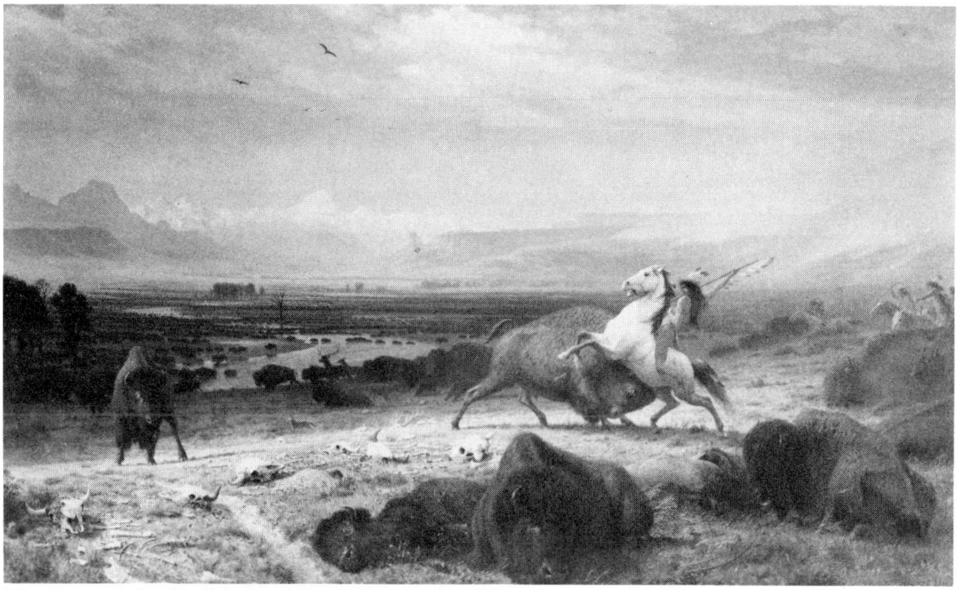

The Last of the Buffalo by Albert Boerstadt. Oil on canvas. The Corcoran Gallery of Art.

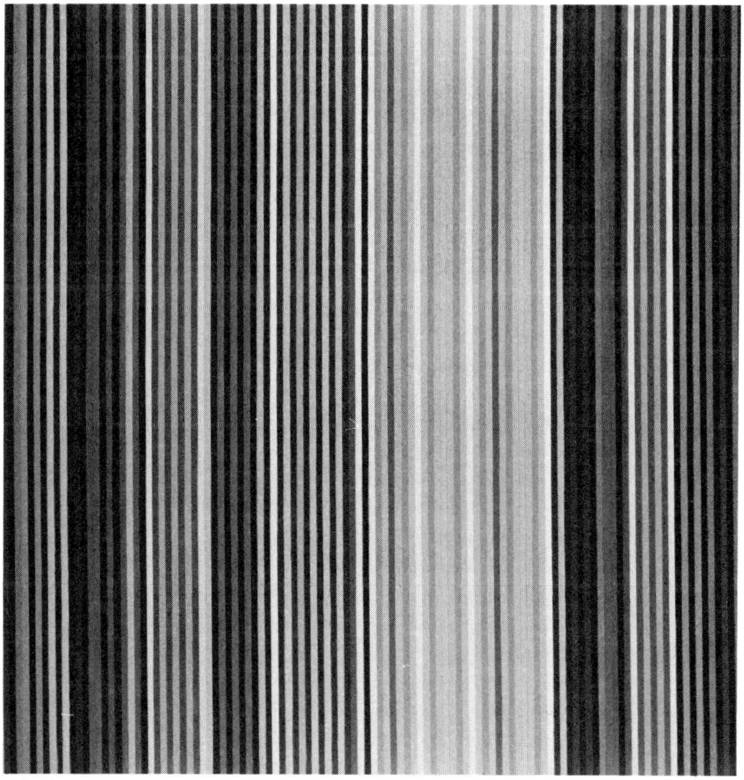

Black Popcorn by Gene Davis. Acrylic on canvas. The Corcoran Gallery of Art.

the Irish poet Yeats, while the poet's painter brother is the center subject of Sloan's *Yeats at Petitpas*; Glackens, Luks, Prendergast, and the rest are all present, and the group culminates in their second generation, George Bellow's *Forty-two Kids*—you can count 'em—skinny-dipping off a rickety-rackety dock.

The continuing twentieth century is not nearly as well represented in the Corcoran as the nineteenth: like most art institutions, the Corcoran made a lot of wrong guesses. There's a good Gottlieb and a radiant Rothko, but nothing like a comprehensive collection of American Abstract Expressionism. The same is true of the succeeding movements, Op, Pop, Minimal, Earthworks, Neo-Realism. There are, all the same, fine paintings by such artists as Pereira, Hans Hoffman, Murch, Bohrod, Kepes, Heliker, Diller, George L. K. Morris, Balcombe Greene, Isobel Bishop, Philip Evergood, Reginald Marsh, Rico Lebrun, and others, all of whom, together, remind the visitor of the excellent work going on in American art before it was overwhelmed by the sheer publicity of Abstract Expressionism.

While American painting is certainly the specialty of the house at the Corcoran, there are other attractions as well. Sculpture includes the famous, or notorious bronze *Turkey* by John Singer Sargent, thought by the irreverent to be his ultimate apotheosis of the Victorian-Edwardian society he made his fortune painting: bosom puffed forward, tail feathers in full rig. There are nice animal bronzes by the great nineteenth-century French *animaleur,* Bayre, and, one of the prizes of the collection from the beginning, the marble *Greek Slave* by Hiram Powers. A daring nude in the context of its time, the *Slave* was for a long time shown to ladies on one day, to gentlemen on another, to avoid embarrassment. Another, lesser-known reward the Corcoran offers the dedicated tramper through these marbled halls is some modest, mild, but quite fine European painting of the nineteenth century, especially a thrilling group of landscapes by Corot, all silvery, greenery, sky and foliage, country roads and grasses. It's where Impressionism didn't quite begin but might well have. In addition, there's a nice group of works by Monticelli and, the surprises of the Corcoran, some late medieval-early Renaissance tapestries, stained glass from Soissons, and an eighteenth-century drawing room, with tennis and monkey motifs, from a Paris private hotel.

The Corcoran is probably most famous nationally, even internationally, for the Biennial Exhibition of American Painting. For many years, this show, along with the Whitney Annual and the Carnegie Biennial in Pittsburgh, was one of the monitors, the guiding lights, giving the general public and indeed the art community itself, valuable hints, suggestions, and indications as to where American art in particular was heading. With the general fragmentation of the American art scene following the decline of Abstract Expressionism, the Corcoran Biennial, like the other national and international shows, has lost, or abandoned, its former role as guide to everyman in his search for art trails. The last Biennial, in 1979, was simply an act of homage to half a dozen Abstract Expressionist and Pop Art masters, long universally recognized, doing very little they had not done before. With the new decade, and a new director, it is possible the Corcoran will attempt to reclaim its former role, in which case the Biennial will again become one of the important exhibitions in this country.

While the Biennial has diminished in importance and interest, however, the Corcoran's over-all exhibition program has grown. It includes, once again, a continuing interest in the work of Washington artists as well as those on the national and international scene. Recent shows have included a dazzling exhibition of tapestries and other art from Senegal, American Indian art, and the work of the Belgian artist Vontongerloo as part of the nationwide manifestation, *Belgium Today.*

The Corcoran is one of the very few major art museums with art schools attached as an integral part of the operation. For the Corcoran, this teaching relationship goes back to the old building, the earliest days of the Corcoran, when Mr. Corcoran decreed that student artists would be allowed to copy the paintings in the collection. For the visitor, this leads to the occasional student exhibition and, usually more rewarding, the occasional faculty show, both of which, if you happen to be there at the right time, can be excellent sources of low-priced but good acquisitions.

Dumbarton Oaks

Dumbarton Oaks 1703 32nd St. NW 232-3101 Tuesday-Sunday: 2-5 Closed Mondays, national holidays, from July 1 through Labor Day, and during "inclement winter weather" Admission free

To most Americans, the name means the site of two crucial international conferences that resulted in the establishment of the United Nations, and indeed this is where those meetings met. Dumbarton Oaks, however, goes back centuries before the U.N. and encompasses two major cultures long since vanished when the U.N. came into being: the Pre-Columbian in the New World and Byzantium in the Old.

The Buildings

The central house of Dumbarton Oaks goes back to 1800, the plot of land to 1702. Standing on the top of Georgetown, overlooking both that old town and Rock Creek ravine, the site was acquired by a diplomatic couple, Mr. and Mrs. Robert Woods Bliss, in 1920. Together and individually they pursued their private passions of collecting: he, Pre-Columbian art (when the field was hardly known to the European and American art worlds); she, the literature and exemplars of floral botany and gardening; both together, the art of Byzantium. Wings have been added to the original building to house both the Byzantine Collection and the gardening library. To house Mr. Bliss's collection of Pre-Columbian art, the architect Philip Johnson created a hidden glass-walled pavilion, which links to the older structures but which is, by itself, one of the architectural gems of this century. Eight transparent cylinders are grouped in a square around an open court, each cylinder presenting, on transparent plinths, the stone carvings, featherwork, gold adornments, and other precious objects of the Pre-Columbian cultures. Marble, bronze, and slate on edge complement the glass, while sunlight, running water, and green foliage all around the outside of the cylinders and in the central mini-court, suggest the ambience of the tropical forests within which the advanced cultures of Mexico, Guatemala, and Peru flourished.

The Collections

Dumbarton Oaks and its collections were given to Harvard University in 1940, although Mr. and Mrs. Bliss continued to contribute to the collections and to the shaping of the place in many ways until their deaths in, respectively, 1962 and 1969. The university preserves, increases, studies, and makes available all three of the basic collections, which have grown considerably since the original gift.

The Byzantine Collection is the center ring at Dumbarton Oaks in terms of depth, breadth, historial importance, and scholarly activity. Byzantium was the Eastern Roman Empire, which survived the Fall of Rome by a thousand years, profoundly changing the art it inherited from ancient Rome, profoundly influencing both the early Renaissance in Italy and Islamic art and architecture after the fall of the Byzantine Empire to the Turks. All of those cultural cross-currents and more are reflected in the Dumbarton Oaks Byzantine Collection. The handbooks available at the sales desk open to the visitor a vast and ancient and incalculably important culture as it is preserved in its art and artifacts.

For centuries the most sophisticated culture in the Western world, Byzantium expressed itself not only in such monumental works as Santa Sophia in Istanbul, but on all scales, including the tiniest in ivory carving and jewelry, as well as in ecclesiastical vessels and vestments. The mosaics Byzantium inherited as an art form from Rome are well represented at Dumbarton Oaks: the visitor easily follows the transition from Roman naturalism in pavement decorations through intermediary stages to the hierarchical stylization of the full Byzantine in the mosaic icon of St. John Chrysostom.

The outreach of the Dumbarton Oaks Byzantine Collection is amply and beautifully demonstrated in two works: a bronze horse, about the size of one on a merry-go-round, from Yemen, a distant Byzantine neighbor, and a little gold man from Roman Gaul, made in the fourth or fifth century, just as that province, roughly modern France, was going barbarian.

Of special interest, among many things, is the Riha Paten, a plate used in the Communion service found in the "treasure" of the Syrian city of Riha. In silver repoussé and gilt, the paten represents the Communion of the Apostles, with Christ seen twice, giving the sacrament to six at a time, the table of the Last Supper clearly a table altar.

The Pre-Columbian collection, housed in the enchanting Philip Johnson glass pavilion, was assembled by Mr. Bliss not to be comprehensive but to be choice—and it is. Every object in it is a thing of beauty. Nothing is there only for its reliquary or historical or geographical value, although all of those elements, of course, are present in many, one or more of them in all. Apparently, the first art object purchased by Mr. Bliss was the Olmec figure of a man in diopside-jadeite; he bought it in Paris in 1912, at which time and place the collecting world was not yet ready for Picasso's interest in African art, let alone the "primitives" of the New World.

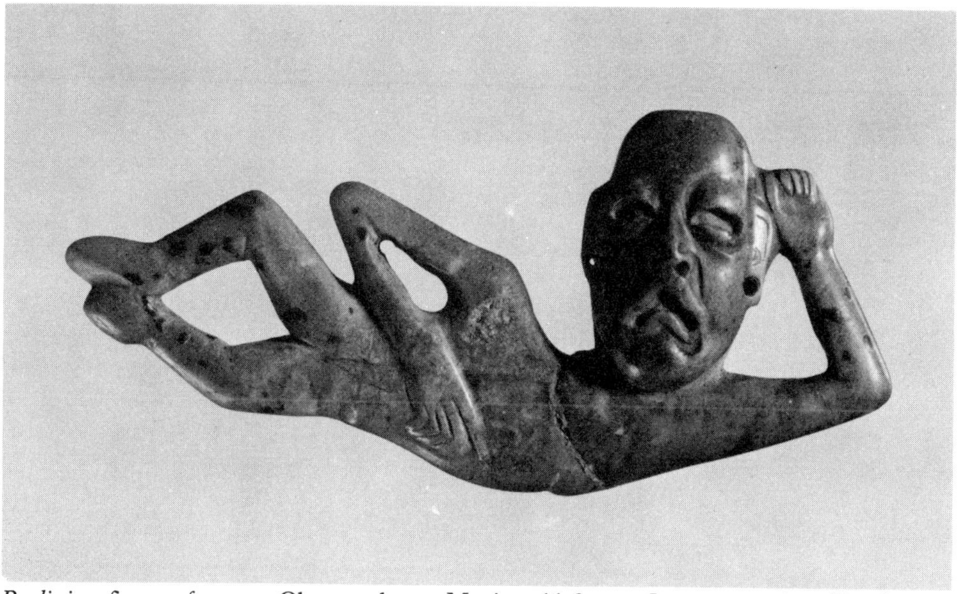

Reclining figure of a man, Olmee culture, Mexico. 11.2cm x 5 cm serpentine. Dumbarton Oaks Collection.

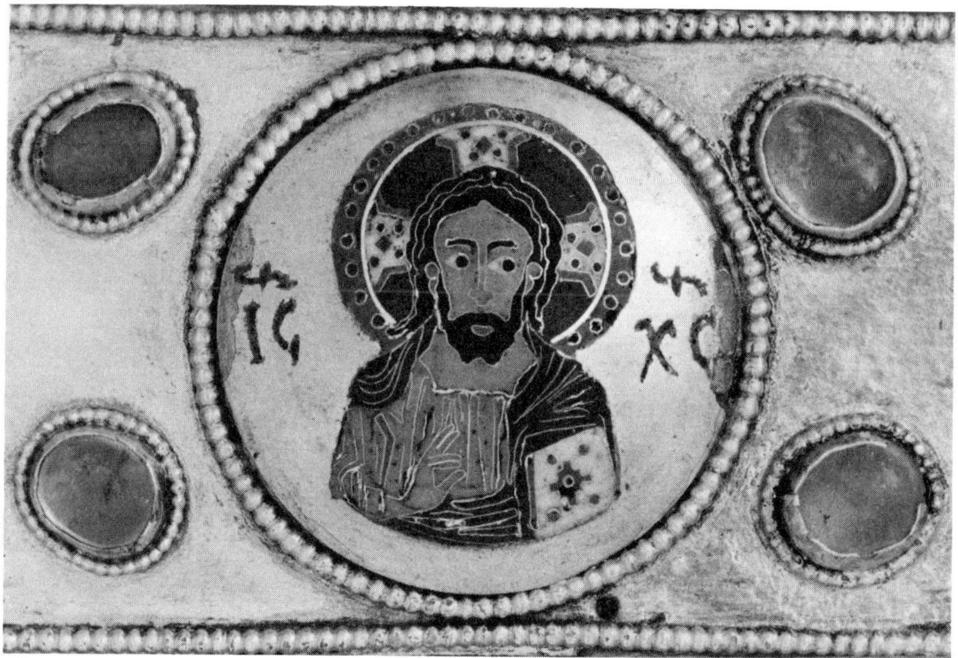

Christ, Constantinople, mid-XI century. Detail, portable icon frame. Dumbarton Oaks Collection.

The collection covers the geography from the Valley of Mexico, through Central America and Panama, Columbia, and Peru. The materials go back at least to 800 B.C., perhaps as far as 1100 B.C. Virtually all the Pre-Columbian cultures are represented, as are all the materials: stone of many kinds, gold, shellwork, and featherwork.

The pieces are grouped by culture in the cylinders of the building. The installation is exquisite.

There is also what Harvard calls the "house collection," at Dumbarton Oaks—the European pictures and objects, the furniture acquired by Mr. and Mrs. Bliss as the accouterments of living. All are still more or less in place as the owners left them, and they are not on public view. The exception is the music room across the front, which one passes on the way in or the way out of the Pre-Columbian pavilion. The one painting the passer-through can get a good look at is the best, El Greco's *Visitation*. The piano has always been in use and still is—in a subscription concert series. It is autographed by Paderewski and was also played by Stravinsky, who here conducted his *Dumbarton Oaks Concerto,* dedicated to Mr. and Mrs. Bliss. In the music room, too, were held the Dumbarton Oaks Conferences.

Freer

Freer Gallery of Art 12th St. and Jefferson Drive, SW 381-6264
Daily: 10-5:30 Closed Christmas Day Admission free

The Freer is one of the great collections of Oriental art in the world and one of the most extensive, including in that term not only the arts of Japan, China, and Korea, but those of Tibet, Southeast Asia, India, the Near East, Asia Minor, Byzantium, and Egypt. In addition there is a splendid collection of American paintings of the turn of the century, with special emphasis on the paintings, prints, and the single interior masterpiece by James McNeill Whistler.

The man who assembled the collections was Charles Lang Freer, a retired railroad-car manufacturer who at 44 retired to devote his life to art. Introduced by Whistler to the Japanese prints that were making a strong impact in Europe, Freer advanced into the more ancient art of Japan and then proceeded to make the Orient his field of study and acquisition, with help from the great Orientalist, Ernest Fenollosa of Harvard and Tokyo.

But Freer remained friends with Whistler all his life, and the Freer holds the largest collection of Whistler's works to be found anywhere, including sets of the etchings pulled by the master for the collector and placed in the boxes that still contain them. In 1906, Freer became the first American to donate to the nation his private art collection, along with funds for a building to house it and a substantial endowment to maintain and expand the collection and to support scholarship in its fields.

The Building

Mr. Freer died three years after ground was broken for the building and four years before the Freer Gallery of Art opened to the public, in 1923. The building is a low structure of gray granite in the style of a Florentine Renaissance palace. Skylighted exhibition galleries surround a

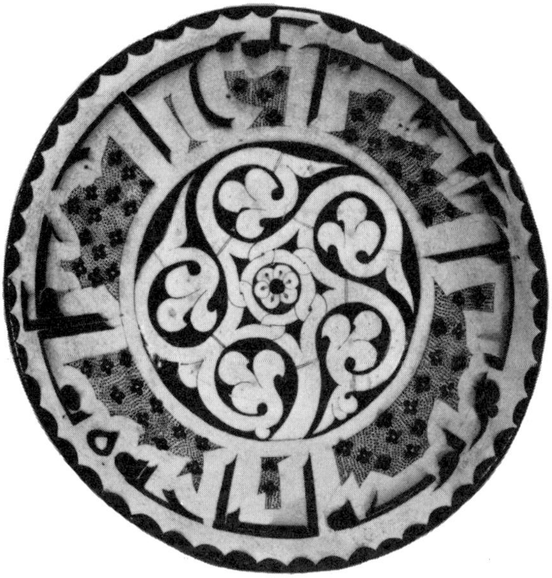

Persian bowl, 10th century. 15½'' diameter. Freer Gallery of Art.

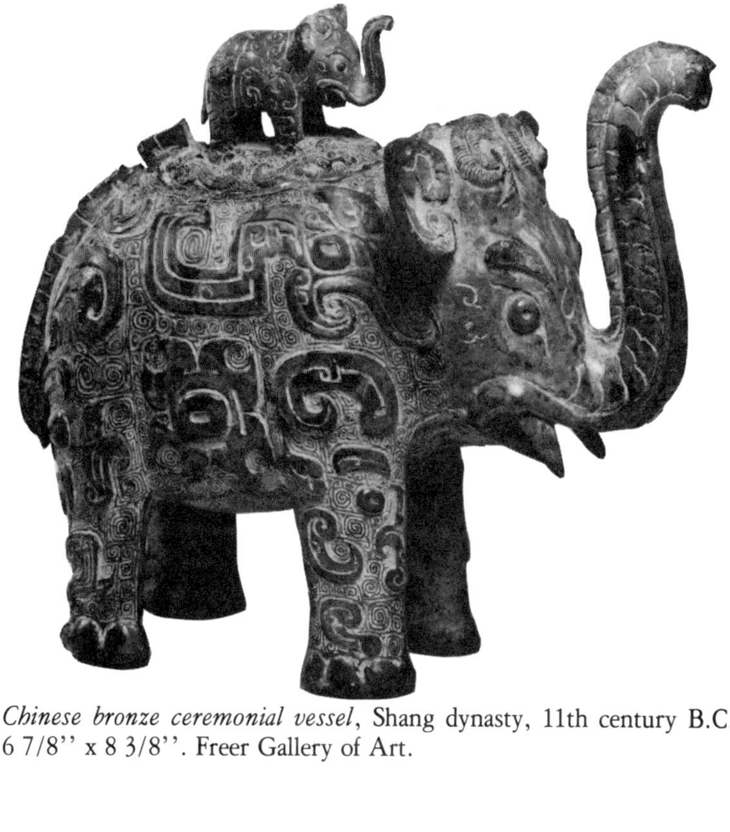

Chinese bronze ceremonial vessel, Shang dynasty, 11th century B.C. 6 7/8'' x 8 3/8''. Freer Gallery of Art.

garden court faced with white marble. Part of the Freer bequest directed the maintenance of an Oriental-style garden. Below the main floor are the offices, workrooms, and storage space.

The Collections

The most spectacular object in the Freer is surely the Peacock Room. This was decorated by Whistler as a setting for his own painting, *Rose and Silver: The Princess from the Land of Porcelain,* which hangs in the room over the fireplace. The room was also to contain a large collection of blue and white porcelain. Whistler, asked to make minor alterations, embarked on a major project which kept growing to the fantastic proportions now seen. In the process the original designer of the room was driven mad, and the central motif of the decorations, the two golden peacocks, is actually a kind of spiritual caricature of the artist and his patron, London shipowner F. R. Leyland.

Besides the extensive Whistler holdings, the American collection contains works by such Whistlerian contemporaries as Dewing, Troyan, Hassam, Homer, Metcalf, Ryder, and Whistler's fellow-expatriate, Sargent.

It is, of course, the Oriental collections that give the Freer its strong position in the international art world. It is impossible to single out individual works as "the best" in any of the national or media categories. Also, the collections can never be on view all at once. However, here are some of the highlights from the collections:

All the Chinese bronzes are fascinating, but those from the Shang dynasty, ca. eleventh century B.C., are particularly so for their age, their technical sophistication, and the intriguing curvilinear surface decorations so suggestive, to American eyes, of the decorative motifs employed by our own Indians of the Pacific Northwest Coast. Vessels in the form of mythical beasts or of small elephants standing on the backs of large elephants enchant all ages.

Similarly, the Japanese objects are extensive and often exquisite, but of special charm is the collection of screens; one screen in particular is covered with representations of fans of all kinds in a remarkable display of art about art. There are lacquered wood sculptures of life size, if you can speak of temple dragons and bodhisattvas as having a particular life size. The scroll paintings from both Japan and China are wonderful, with the Japanese showing perhaps more of a touch of human insouciance or flipness as compared to the formal informality of Chinese landscapes being contemplated by philosophers.

There are marvelous Persian miniatures, illustrative of love stories and royal entertainments, but the most compelling Persian art of the Freer is much older: a richly gilded Sasanian silver dish of the fourth century A.D., showing a king hunting a boar, all in low relief and gilded; and, earlier still, a matched pair of Achaemenid golden goats, sixth to fifth century B.C., highly stylized with bands of fine gold wire wound around their waists, originally used as handles on a jar. Of all the miniatures from Persia, probably the most interesting is a portrait from the 1400s, possibly by Bihzad, the greatest of Persian painters, and bearing an amazing resemblance to a painting of Gentile Bellini now in Boston.

Korea has bronzes, but the distinctive objects in the collection are the ceramics, shapes related to but differing from the classic Chinese shapes, and, above all, the incredible, seemingly breathed on, peach-blossom glaze of so many of the domestic-size vessels.

The bronzes and brasswork of India are shimmering in surface and distinguish themselves from European bronzes because so many of them depict figures in dance, highlighting physical tension, grace, and movement caught in its flow that are a rare combination in Europe.

Finally, the great treasures in the Egyptian-Syrian section are scriptural, the fourth-fifth-century manuscript of the Gospels of all Four Evangelists and a third-century Egyptian manuscript on papyrus of the Minor Prophets of the Old Testament.

Tours The Freer features walk-in tours, Mon.-Fri. at 2.

Transportation Of all the museums included in the Smithsonian Institution, the Freer Gallery is closest to the Smithsonian station of the Metro subway system, on the Blue Line.

Hirshhorn Hirshhorn Museum and Sculpture Garden Independence Avenue at 8th Street, SW 381-5911 Daily: 10:30-5:30 Summer: 10-9 Closed Christmas Day Admission free

Beginning in the mid-1930s, Joseph H. Hirshhorn, New York stockbroker and investor, built an art collection that rapidly became one of the legends of the American art world. Reputed—falsely—to rush into dealers' galleries and buy entire exhibitions, Hirshhorn assembled the most extensive private collection of twentieth-century American art in existence. Of particular interest was an overwhelming sculpture collection of both American and European works from the nineteenth century to the present, with the present always advancing with the calendar. To his home in Greenwich, Conn., came art lovers by the hundreds, mostly for institutional benefit showings, to see an extraordinary collection which they realized was barely the tip of the iceberg of the Hirshhorn holdings.

Even so, that American art world was ill-prepared for the sheer cornucopia quality of the collection when, in October 1974, the Hirshhorn Museum and Sculpture Garden opened its doors. Some 850 objects from a total of about 6,000—since increased—were on view. They included many of the masterworks of nineteenth- and twentieth-century sculpture and painting, European as well as American. Seemingly everyone of any consequence in the last century was represented, often in unusual depth. Of equal interest were the extensive groups of the works of individual artists known, heard of, but rarely seen in any breadth. It came as a surprise, too, to those who thought of the Hirshhorn Collection as exclusively concerned with modern art, that the sculpture includes Hittite, archaic Greek, Etruscan, and a good selection of Benin bronzes. Not surprisingly, all those past schools show formal and/or emotive affinities with one or more manifestations of nineteenth- and twentieth-century sculpture.

The Building

Like so much else about the Hirshhorn donation of the collection and contribution toward erecting the building to house it, the building itself was a cause of controversy. The circular design by architect Gordon Bunshaft seemed so blunt, so stark, so at odds with the classical and Victorian Gothic architecture of the Mall. A few years later, with the Air and Space Museum next door and the National Gallery's East Building across the Mall, the Hirshhorn is not so solitary in its modernity of look. And there was never any question about the workability of the building. It works like a charm. Within the almost all-encompassing walls, the sawed-off cylinder of the building rests on four great piers: in effect, the ground level is open, except for a glass-enclosed reception area off Independence Avenue. The main galleries are in the two circular floors above the open space, both reached by escalator. The escalator also carries the visitor to the floor below ground level, where there are galleries for temporary exhibitions, a small but choice sales shop and the cloak room.

The plan is simplicity itself. On those two main gallery floors, the inner circle is small sculpture, the outer circle paintings. The sculpture galleries are open to the sculpture plaza on ground level, with a pool and fountain sufficiently off-center from the building to provoke visual interest.

The sculpture plaza in the center of the hollow cylinder spills over into the adjacent areas within the walls which constitute the pleasantest place in Washington to have an outdoor lunch in season. Toward the Mall is a staircase leading to an under-the-street passage to the sunken sculpture garden, which can also be approached by simply crossing the street, Jefferson Drive. The sunken site solved the problem of the need for a sculpture garden for the many large, even monumental, pieces, made for the outdoors, and, on the other hand, the need to maintain unbroken the majestic sweep of the Mall from the Capitol to the Washington Monument. The sculpture garden offers numerous changes of level, foliage as space dividers, water, and, of course, the ever-changing effects of sunlight, cloud shadow, even rain and snow.

The Collection

The most spectacular installation at the Hirshhorn is the one in the sculpture garden, no matter what changes are made from time to time in the pieces actually on view. At least two major works will aways be there, barring cataclysmic change. One is the set of four relief sculptures in bronze by Matisse set against the garden wall, larger than life and depicting the nude female back through changes from relative realism to relative abstraction. The other is the great Rodin, slightly larger than life, *The Burghers of Calais,* depicting an incident in the Hundred Years' War when the town fathers of the channel port surrendered themselves to the besieging British troops, with hanging ropes around their necks to buy the safety of the town and their fellow-townspeople.

There are more Rodins, in the garden and in the building, most notably outside the upward-thrusting Balzac, the novelist in the nude, as self-assured and mobile as any of his heroes. Picasso's funny *Baby Carriage,* made of junk cast into bronze, is in the garden, as are major

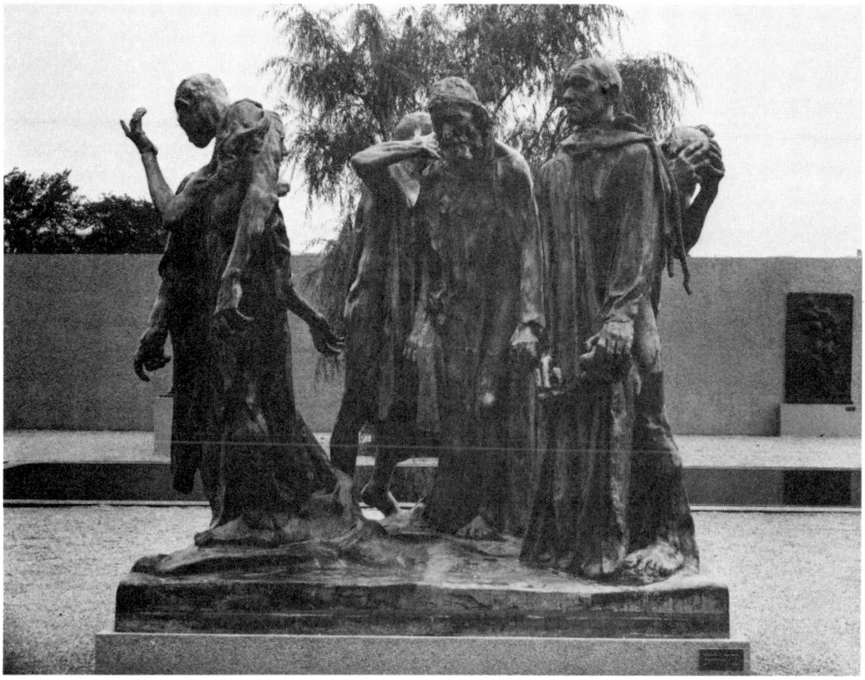

The Burghers of Calais by Auguste Rodin. 82½'' x 95'' x 78'' bronze. Hirshhorn Museum and Sculpture Garden.

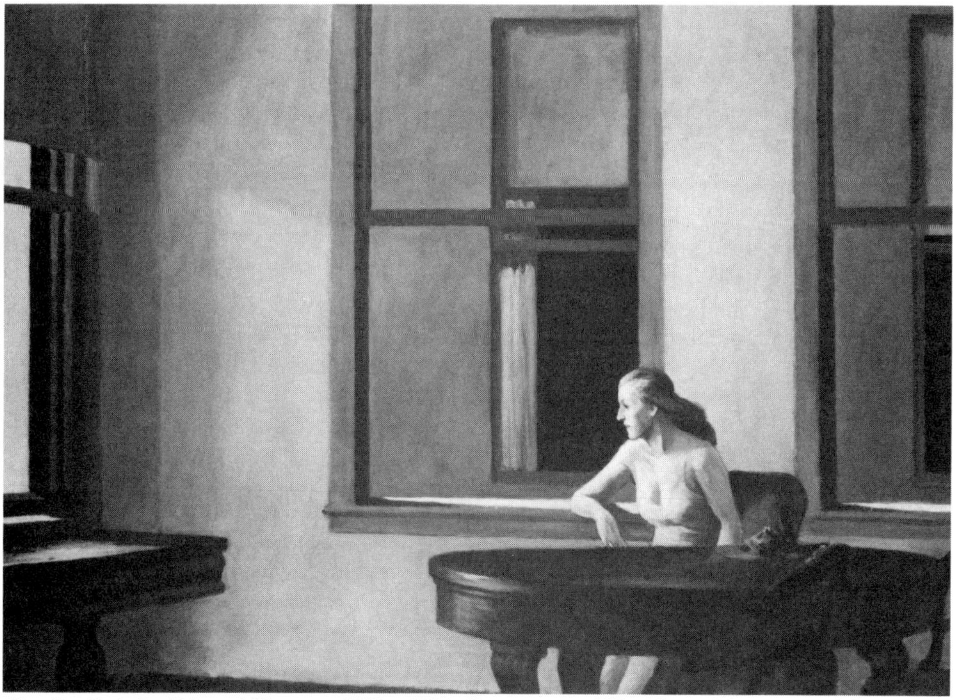

City Sunlight by Edward Hopper. 28'' x 40'' oil on canvas. Hirshhorn Museum and Sculpture Garden.

works by Calder, David Smith, Henry Moore, Lipchitz, Noguchi, Brancusi: to name it is to find it somewhere at the Hirshhorn. In the walls of the tunnel connecting garden with plaza are set two bronze reliefs by the great American painter, Thomas Eakins, one of Washington crossing the Delaware with considerable more credibility than is visible in Emanuel Leutze's famous painting, and the beginning of the battle of Trenton. These are a harbinger of the fact that the Hirshhorn has more works by Eakins than anyplace in the country except the Philadelphia Museum in the artist's hometown.

Facing the Mall, a long, slender George Rickey *Three Red Lines*, stands as an emblem at the entrance to the plaza and keeps time as a kind of random silent metronome. An enigmatic bronze *Cardinal* by Manzu performs the same function inside the circle, facing the fountain.

Because sculpture is nowhere, this side of the Bargello in Florence, as bountifully available as it is at the Hirshhorn, it is easy to take the sculptural plunge and think of the Hirshhorn as primarily a museum of sculpture. It isn't. Roughly, there are twice as many paintings as there are sculptures, yet the amount of sculpture so far exceeds that of most American art museums as to create the false impression of sculptural hegemony.

One of the special delights in the sculpture holdings is that they include so many three-dimensional works by artists we normally think of—and who thought of themselves—as primarily, even exclusively, painters. Eakins has been mentioned. The two bronze reliefs are not the only sculptures by that arguably greatest of American artists in the Hirshhorn. Degas, who only turned to sculpture as a substitute for painting, particularly as his eyesight began to fade, and whose sculptural works, modeled in wax, were not cast in bronze until after his death, is also well represented. So is Daumier, best known for his lithographic cartoons of nineteenth-century French manners and morals and political vicissitudes; to help his caricature of politicians, he modeled them and drew from the busts and figures. Later these were cast into bronze, and the Hirshhorn has platoons of them, including the immortal *Ratapoil*, an invented character embodying the worst of French rightist inclinations. Similarly, there are sculptures by Matisse and Picasso, by John Singer Sargent, Modigliani and Bonnard.

But the main line of modern sculpture is more than adequately represented: Lipchitz, Brancusi, Arp, the Constructivists, the Futurists, the Expressionists, of course the Cubists, the Geometricians, those who never entirely gave up the figure: Nadelman, Robus, Flanagan, Gonzalez, Giacometti, Arp, Epstein in both the *Visitation* and the head of Joseph Conrad, among others.

In painting, the Hirshhorn is probably best known for its splendid collection of advanced work from the Abstract Expressionists on up. But there is much earlier work of special value that is not so readily available—for instance, the many, many paintings of Louis Eilshemius, now almost forgotten, perhaps, but in his time a prophet and teacher to young artists in New York.

Another virtue of the Hirshhorn Collection is that it never accepted the popular point of view that artistic virtue lay with one advanced artistic mode only. Throughout the years when works by De Kooning and Pollock, Albers and Frank Stella were being acquired, Hirshhorn kept buying the best—and often the best paintings—of painters suddenly out of fashion like Jack Levine, Ben Shahn, Raphael Soyer, Philip Evergood, and even Pollock's teacher, Thomas Hart Benton.

Besides those already mentioned, some of the highlights of the Hirshhorn to look for are:

Kaethe Kollwitz's bronze self-portrait, a face of total resignation and sublimation;

Ernst Barlach's *Old Woman Laughing*, an unexpected companion piece to that sculptor's better-known *Singing Man*;

Stanton MacDonald-Wright's *Conception Synchrony,* in which that pioneer American abstractionist, working before World War I, presented pure color shapes remarkably like work of the 1960s by much younger artists who had never heard of him;

John Sloan's *McSorley's Saturday Night,* for an evocation of what was once the best-known saloon in New York and the same painter's *Carmine Theater,* for the only depiction of an ash can by a member of the Ash Can School;

Some of the small Henry Moore sculptures, such as *Family Group* and especially *Rocking Chair No. 2,* accompanied by a sheet of drawings for the piece.

Etienne Hajdu's perfect evocation of *Adolescence* in flat, patterned marble, complete with highly stylized ponytail;

Europa and the Bull by Lipchitz in bronze, by Reuben Nakian in terra-cotta, to see the difference between the men, the media, and the methods when addressing a common theme;

Salvador Dali's *Skull of Zurbaran,* a trick painting that should strengthen your preference for Zurbaran;

The Stuart Davis classic *Rapt at Rappaport's,* but also his earlier *The Terminal,* in which he was still dealing with recognizable scenes but treating their components in the neon-jazz fashion that was to make him such a delightful member of the pre-Abstract Expressionist art scene;

Jack Levine's elegantly savage *Reception in Miami,* the absolute last word on the Duke and Duchess of Windsor;

And finally the amazing combination of both the painting and the sculpture, *Delusions of Grandeur* by Rene Magritte of torso inside torso inside torso.

Exhibitions

The Hirshhorn pursues a vigorous exhibition program in its own field of modern art, European and American. Recent exhibitions have included a very full Joan Miro retrospective, an unexpected look at Brancusi as a photographer, a review of the Latin American painter, Fernando Botero, and a fascinating resurrection of the 1950s in New York painting.

In mounting exhibitions of its own and also in taking in exhibitions from other institutions, the Hirshhorn has and uses the enormous advantage of its own extensive holdings of so many artists in areas of its interests. In addition to the special exhibitions presented, usually, in the below-ground-level galleries, the Hirshhorn frequently mounts less-heralded mini-exhibitions of a single artist within the regular galleries from its own permanent collection.

Transportation The Hirshhorn Museum and Sculpture Garden is a few blocks north and west of Metro subway station Federal Center South, on the Blue Line.

Library of Congress The Library of Congress First Street between Independence Ave. and East Capitol Street SE 426-5000 Daily: 9-9:30 Closed Christmas Day Admission free

The Library of Congress was created by the Congress in 1800 with an appropriation of $5,000 to buy books and furnish "an appropriate apartment for containing them." In the War of 1812, the Library was burned by the British along with the Capitol. Ex-President Jefferson offered his own library, probably the best in private hands in the new nation, in 1815.

The Building The Library remained in that "appropriate apartment" in the Capitol until the opening of the Main Building in 1897. There are two annexes, one behind the Main, the other across Independence Avenue from the Main. The Main Building is the city's masterpiece of Victorian Renaissance architecture and may be the most dazzlingly successful work ever done by the Army Corps of Engineers. The Great Hall is one of the great spaces left us by a more spacious age, beautifully articulated with staircases, balustrades, colonnades, arches, lunettes, and other features. Statuary, murals, and brass insets in the walls commemorate the arts, the signs of the zodiac, civic virtues, and an occasional Greek goddess. Whether seen from a scholar's desk on the floor or from the Visitors' Gallery, the Main Reading Room is breathtaking.

Prints This is probably the world's finest and most extensive library, but what concerns us here is its superb collection of prints and photographs in its division of that name. There are over 70,000 prints in the collection dating from the fifteenth to the twentieth centuries. Many of the rarest were submitted for copyright in the nineteenth century. The collection includes very rare nineteenth-century posters, among them the famous "24-sheets" advertising the circus and intended for the broadsides of barns. The Library has been active in putting on exhibitions of contemporary American prints, from which it has bought examples, thus maintaining one of the great print collections in the world.

Photographs, which came to the division naturally, as a kind of print, document the entire history of photography, back to the callotypes of Fox Talbot and the daguerrotypes of Mathew Brady. The efforts of Brady and his colleagues to cover the Civil War are well represented as are the early Western photos of William Henry Jackson and Timothy O'Sullivan. The Stieglitz group and the photographers of the Farm Security Administrations are here, along with the photo files of *Look* magazine. Motion pictures have been cared for in the division ever since the *Edison Kinetoscopic Record of a Sneeze* was deposited for copyright in 1894.

Exhibitions Needless to say, only representative selections from this photographic and print gold mine are on view at any one time, but the new Madison Annex has increased available exhibition space and, it is hoped, will increase the amount of the work on view. Almost always there is an exhibition of photos by members of some professional association, usually journalistic, and an exhibition of prints by individuals or groups.

African Art

Museum of African Art 318 A St. NE 547-6222 Monday-Friday: 11-5 Saturday and Sunday: 12-5 Closed Thanksgiving and Christmas day Admission free

The Museum of African Art, founded in 1964 by Warren Robbins, a former Foreign Service officer, is the only American museum exclusively devoted to African art.

The Buildings The museum occupies half a dozen houses in its Capitol Hill block. The one at 318 A St. was once the home of Frederick Douglass, the escaped slave, writer, lecturer, diplomat, and friend of Abraham Lincoln. That house and the one next door comprise the exhibition space, while the others house offices, an African boutique that offers some of the all-time bargains in museums sales shops, and a restaurant featuring African foods.

The Collection The museum's own collection is not enormous, but Robbins has been extremely effective in borrowing existing collections, including those assembled by Eliot Elisofon, the late, great *Life* photographer, and by Chaim Gross, the sculptor, whose revival of wood carving as a medium for modern art led him naturally to African sculpture.

The 500 or so pieces the museum owns are shown on a rotating basis with highly imaginative themes and installations. The visitor is as likely as not to come across a group of Washington schoolchildren—which means mostly black—gaining familiarity with their ancestral heritage, not just by looking and listening but by wearing dance costumes, dancing, and playing drums and other African musical instruments.

Robbins became interested in African art while doing cross-cultural research focused on the impact of African art upon early-twentieth-century European artists such as the German Expressionists, Picasso, and Alexander Calder. One gallery memorializes that origin of the museum in a permanent, and highly persuasive comparison between the works of, for example, Calder, Picasso, Klee, and Schmidt-Rottluff and African masks, sculptures, and decorative motifs.

Another permanent installation more or less reproduces the study of Frederick Douglass, with furnishings which are either Douglass's own or identical objects from the period.

In the process of his cross-cultural studies, however, Warren Robbins quickly came to realize the aesthetic merit and historic importance of African art in its own right—and this is the focus of the museum. Perhaps the most dramatic single wall in an American art museum is the one at the Museum of African Art that displays a large group of headdresses of the antelope worn and danced in by the Bambara people in Mali at planting and harvesting times. The most fascinating collection within the collection is the assemblage of tiny bronze sculptures used as gold weights by the Ashanti people; they illustrate people and animals and such penetrating folk sayings as "The hen also knews when day breaks, but she lets the rooster announce it."

Exhibitions

From the diplomatic point of view—and Robbins was a diplomat before he turned museum founder—the Museum of African Art could hardly have come into existence at a better time or in a better place: an important capital in a period of growing African ruie of African nations. A slow but steady series of exhibitions has been and continues to be provided by the new African nations anxious to present their works and their national soul to the Americans. Typical of the shows here was the recent mounting of works by six nineteenth-century American black artists, at least one of whom had always been assumed by most art critics to be white.

But for many visitors, by far the most compelling and most instantly instructive exhibition is the permanent slide-tape show created from the hundreds of color photographic slides given to the museum by Elisofon. The photography, of course, is that of a master; in addition, the slides are so presented that they fade into each other, creating a continuous context. Some visitors leave convinced they've seen a movie. The sound track, in addition to its lecture aspect, contains the chants and drumbeats of the dances illustrated, rain on a straw roof, the hoofbeats and growls of animals, the night cries of birds and insects, wind in the palms, waters over rapids.

Tours

Tours are available to groups by calling (202) 547-7424.

The museum has been acquired as a bureau of the Smithsonian Institution, which insures its permanence; it is scheduled, at some future indefinite date, to move down to a new building on The Mall, but many of its friends hope that move will be a long way off.

Air & Space

National Air and Space Museum Independence Avenue between 4th and 7th Sts. SW 381-4222 Daily: 10-5:30 Summer hours: 10-9 Closed Christmas Day Admission free

The National Air and Space Museum commemorates the one effort that brought united national support through the tumultuous decade of the 1960s. The museum contains a record, through the actual planes and other equipment, of the swift development of the age of flight from the Wright Brothers *Flyer* through the Space Lab and beyond.

The Building

The building created to house this remarkable record of achievement is remarkable in itself—appropriately—and will well repay any attention given it. The unusual problem of suspending bulky and weighty objects, like airplanes and rockets, from an interior frame was elegantly solved by architect Gyo Obato who simply followed the line of logic in letting in as much sky as possible for an activity that largely takes place there and in spreading the weight stresses as far as possible around the structure.

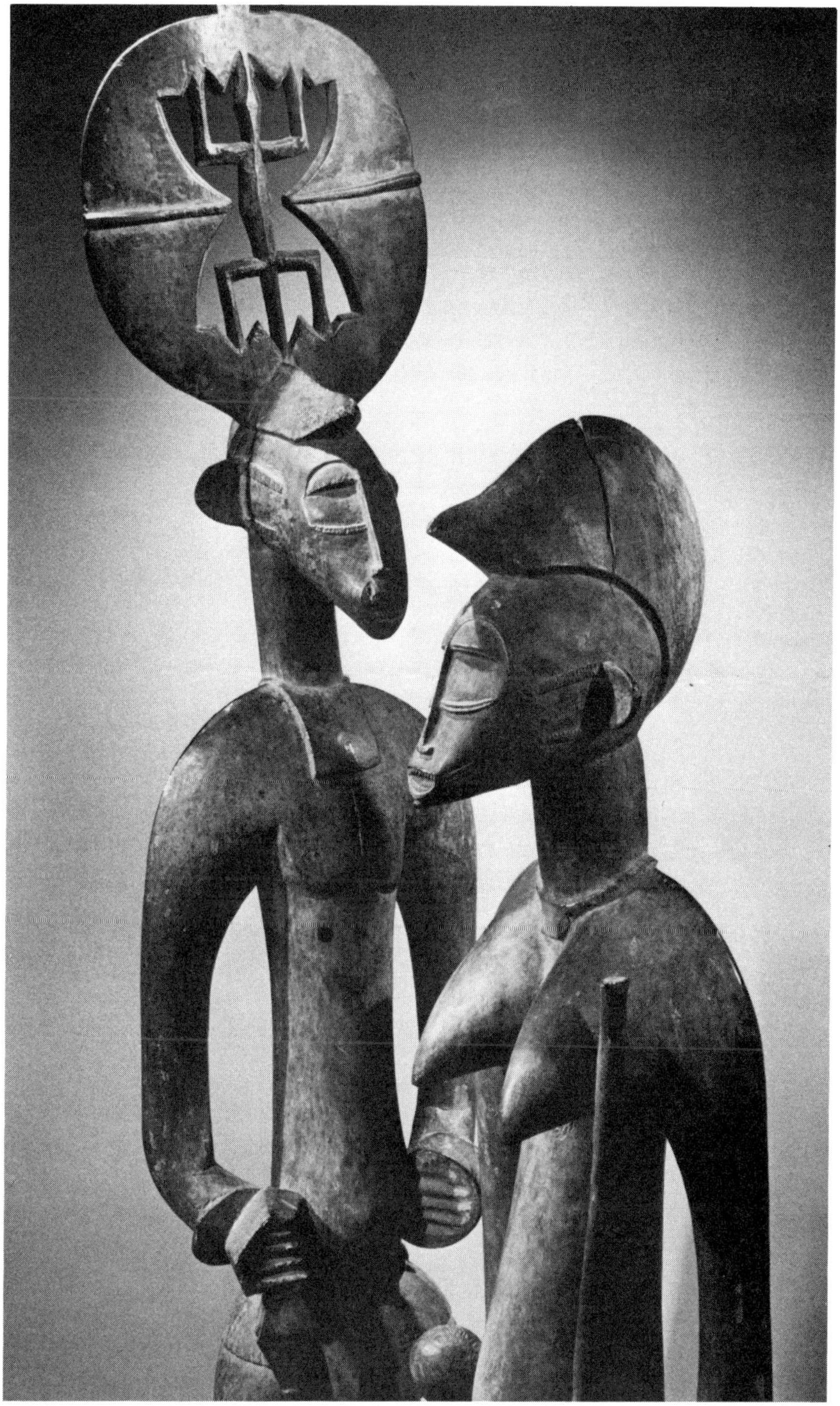

Deble, Senufo, Ivory Coast. 57½'' rhythm pounders. Museum of African Art.

The Collection The primary collections of the museum, of course, are the ships, the balloons, and the accouterments of flying, all of them mostly beyond the scope of this book. (It is within our scope, though, to call the visitor's attention to a marvelous reconstruction of an actual flying field and an actual incident of World War I just before the Armistice: the re-creation is a work of art itself and easily overlooked among all the Mars and moon material of the museum.) The NASA program designed to explore space did an unusual thing. It hired the curator of paintings at the National Gallery of Art, the late H. Lester Cooke, to set up and run a program of art documentation of the program. The result is the permanent art collection of the museum—sketches, watercolors, oils, and sculptures of events leading to and from the nation's ventures into space. Artists such as Jamie Wyeth, Mitchell Jamieson, Richard Lippold, and Norman Rockwell went to Cape Kennedy for lift-offs, to the decks of far-flung carriers for splash-downs, and recorded what they saw and felt. The program was rare among government projects since the New Deal, when art was all over the place, and the results are well worth the miniscule investment.

The paintings of the program are augmented from time to time by, for instance, color photographs of the earth taken from great heights, including the height of the moon.

Transportation The National Air and Space Museum is readily available from the Federal Center South station on the Metro subway's Blue Line.

National Collection

National Collecton of Fine Arts 8th and G Streets NW 628-4422
Daily: 10-5:30 Closed Christmas Day Admission free

The National Collection of Fine Arts has suffered as many perils as Pauline. An early version of the museum was destroyed by fire in the last days of the Civil War. Later, it even lost its name, "The National Gallery of Art," when Congress conferred that title on what was then the Mellon Collection. Housed for years in dim, hard-to-find quarters in the Smithsonian's Museum of Natural History, behind the largest elephant ever captured, the NCFA seemed like a particularly dark and dusty corner of "the nation's attic," as the Smithsonian was called. Then suddenly, like Cinderella, the NCFA came to new life, occupying one of the handsomest and most historically important art buildings in Washington, and presenting an always stimulating, often first-rate program of special exhibitions.

The Building The new NCFA is housed in the north half of the Old Patent Office Building, a Washington landmark, which, like many such, had been scheduled to be destroyed for the sake of a parking garage. Popular opposition enlisted the aid of key congressmen and of President Eisenhower to save it. The building was turned over to the Smithsonian in 1958 to house both the NCFA and the newly created, though long planned, National Portrait Gallery. Ten years later the two institutions opened their doors to the public and revealed a long forgotten architectural beauty that had been totally obscured by "temporary" partitions erected when the structure was occupied by the Civil Service Commission.

The building is, in fact, one of the triumphs of Greek Revival architecture in America. The facades suggest the Parthenon on the theory that since the gift of Invention was America's particular genius, the Patent Office is thus a kind of shrine. Inside there is a sense of proportion and of variety in the decorative elements and in the spaces. The Granite Gallery, now dedicated to changing exhibitions of works from the permanent collection, is a wonderful room full of great, thick columns reminding us that this is a load-bearing masonry building. The Lincoln Gallery, which runs the entire east side of the building, is indeed the NCFA's Grand Gallery. Its name commemorates Lincoln's Second Inaugural Ball which was held here. During the Civil War the still-not-quite-completed building was used as a military hospital for the wounded from nearby Virginia. Among those who nursed the troops in these halls were Walt Whitman and Clara Barton, who went on to found the American Red Cross.

The Collections

The NCFA lost some of its holdings before it ever reached its handsome quarters. Its substantial decorative-arts pieces were given to the Smithsonian's Museum of History and Technology, many of its historically important American portraits to the new National Portrait Gallery. Still, it has enough left to offer an extensive view of nineteenth- and twentieth-century American art and, in the Gellatly Collection, a view not of European painting and sculpture as such but rather of those fields as they were expressed in "the taste of the time" of an early twentieth-century gentleman of sophistication and means.

Among the European works of such interest, not all from Gellatly, are the early-sixteenth-century *Madonna and Child* attributed to Bernardino Luini, a Flemish *Adoration of the Kings* of the same period, an earlier Flemish *Entombment,* and especially the Rubens *Madonna and Child.*

Mr. Gellatly was not exclusively European in his art interests, nor were some of his fellow donors. He himself is responsible for the collection's remarkable group of paintings by the American mystical painter, Albert Pinkham Ryder, 17 in all, including *Jonah* and *The Flying Dutchman.* He also gave the nation a dozen paintings by the Impressionist John Twachtman, 15 by Childe Hassam, and 23 by Abbott Thayer, who hasn't been much favored in recent decades but who, nevertheless, remains a powerful witness of popular sentiment in his time.

The NCFA owns the definitive collection of Indian paintings by George Catlin, the Philadelphia artist who, seeing a delegation of Indians en route for treaty talks, was fired with the ambition to capture the Indians on canvas before they inevitably vanished in the wake of the American expansion. The 445 Catlins are represented by a selection in the Lincoln Gallery.

Another unusual strength in the American holdings is the entire collection of art and its tools left in his Florentine studio by nineteenth-century classical sculptor, Hiram Powers. There is a special gallery for Powers's works.

Probably the most important single painting in the NCFA is the magnificent Winslow Homer, *High Cliff, Coast of Maine,* painted in 1894 when Homer was at the peak of his command of sea, mist, and light along that stern and rock-bound coast.

In twentieth-century painting of its own country, the NCFA's greatest stroke was its acquisition of the S. C. Johnson Collection, also known as "Art Now USA," which was assembled by New York art dealer Lee Nordness for a tour in this country and abroad. The 51 paintings were selected consciously and conscientiously to give as complete a representation as possible of American painting as of 1962. That was the "Now" of the title. It is now, of course, a "Then," but the collection holds up well. It is a broad overview of the field. Most of the Abstract Expressionists are present, but so are dozens of artists who painted in a different mode: Isabel Bishop, for example, Jack Levine, Ben Shahn, Abraham Rattner, and Paul Cadmus.

Exhibitions

The new lease on life given the NCFA by its move to the Old Patent Office Building actually began before that move with a series of brilliant exhibitions of major American twentieth-century artists put on by David W. Scott. His successor as director, Joshua Taylor, has continued and broadened that new tradition, reaching back into the nineteenth century and often enough bringing to our attention worthwhile "forgotten" artists of the past. Two such shows recently celebrated John R. Grabach, a twentieth-century painter with affinities to Bellows and Twachtman, and art commissioned for Federal buildings in the 1970s.

Special galleries for children—and adults—are "Discover" and "Explore," dedicated to showing visitors the problems and possibilities of the elements in art.

Transportation

The NCFA is across the street from the Gallery Place exit on the Metro subway's Red Line. It is also served by a free-of-charge double-decker London bus leaving regularly from the Museum of History and Technology.

National Gallery

The National Gallery of Art Constitution Ave. at 6th St. NW 737-4215 Monday-Saturday: 10-5, April 1 through Labor Day: 10-9 Sunday: 12-9 Closed: Christmas Day Admission free

The Buildings

The National Gallery of Art opened in 1941 in its beautiful neoclassic building designed by the last great neoclassic architect, John Russell Pope. Like the best of neoclassic architecture, among which it ranks, the building, now called the West Building, is serene and majestic, its columns and proportions invoking the majesty of the ancient Rome that the American Republic has always considered its ancestor. The Tennessee pink marble of the fabric of the building was carefully installed in subtle color gradations from bottom to top, an effect best observed in the rain. The dome of the central rotunda on the main floor is supported by great columns of green marble centered on a pool and fountain surmounted by the bronze statue of *Mercury* by Giambologna. The two main corridors or sculpture halls, off the rotunda lead to the spacious Garden Courts, east and west, with some 70 galleries off the corridors displaying the art in generously proportioned but not overwhelming

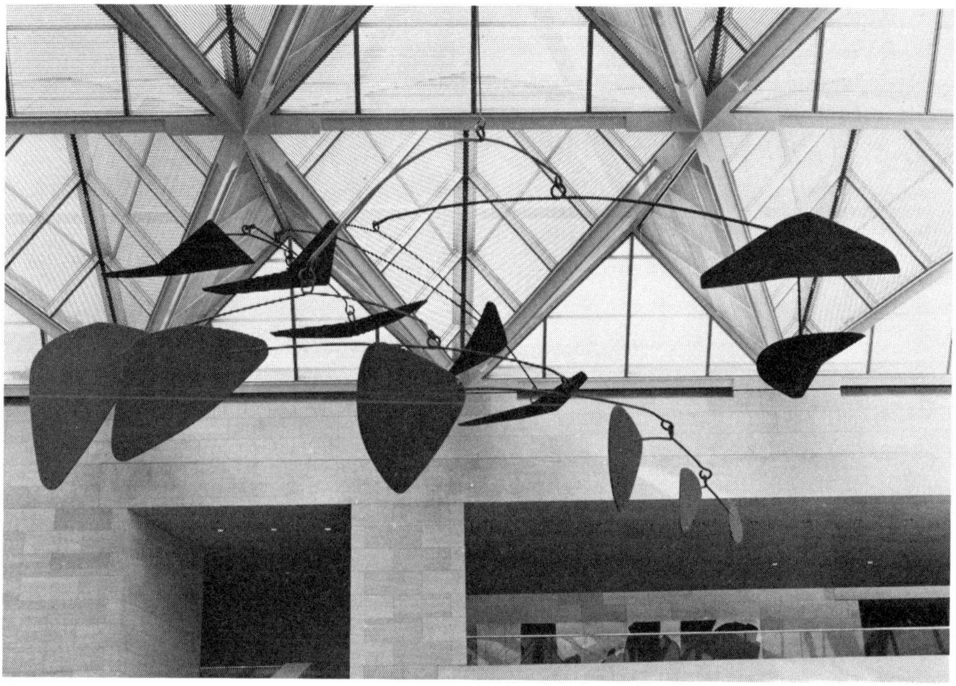

Interior view of East Building, National Gallery. Alexander Calder Mobile atop.

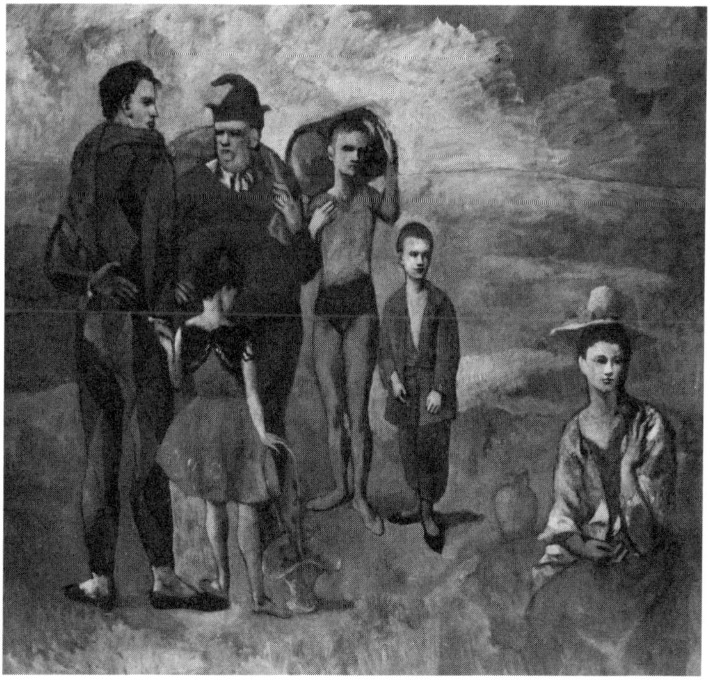

Family of Saltimbanques 1905 by Pablo Picasso. 83 3/4'' x 90 3/8'' oil on canvas. National Gallery of Art.

space. The effect of all of this is to induce a certain reverence for art and, perhaps more important, a sense of balance and order, the intrinsic qualities of classic art. What the visitor seeks and finds in the paintings is also found in their setting.

The East Building, opened in June 1978, was designed by the great modern architect, I. M. Pei, and, in a totally different look, nevertheless captures the same classical qualities so evident in the original building. The East Building is sheathed in the same Tennessee pink marble as the older structure, and its attic lines are the same height, but the look is a whole new world of architecture and space. If the West Building is based on the circle, the square, the rectangle in assorted combinations, the East Building is based on the triangle in what seems every conceivable variation. The plot of land for the new building, set aside by Congress in the original establishing legislation, is a trapezoid created by the conjunction of the grid of the Mall with the diagonal of Pennsylvania Avenue, the famed "Main Street of the nation," linking the Capitol with the Treasury and the White House. Pei split the trapezoid into two triangles, sharing a common side, one for the new study center, the first time an essentially academic, art-historical operation has been incorporated into a major art museum, the other for exhibition and public space. The two basic triangles are joined by a third, the glass roof, itself a honeycomb of triangles. The floors are composed of triangular units, even the columns are triangles, and the elevators are contained in double triangles of space. The triangular space of the exhibition hall is flooded with light through the ceilings, including those of the three towers of exhibition space, and through the great glass walls and windows everywhere encountered, in sharp distinction from the windowless walls of the West Building. The exigencies of formal exhibition space are met in a series of "pods," starting on the basement level and going all the way up to and into those towers. But the public, "non-pod" space invites the visitor to move through it, to change levels by way of stairs and moving stairs, to experience constantly changing space relationships beneath the constantly changing configurations of Alexander Calder's last giant-sized mobile, hung from the space frame of glass above all the framed space.

The pods are flexible and can be as elaborate as the basement-level one has been for the Dresden and Arts of the Pacific exhibitions, as intimate as the tower room was for the Matisse show, which, along with a few paintings, featured the master's books and the prints of the "Jazz" series.

There is an underground "Connecting Link" between the two buildings which contains the superb bookstore, two good restaurants—by museum standards, fabulous—a waterfall in the shape of another triangle, and a "people mover" in both directions.

The Collections

The National Gallery of Art is not a universal museum, like the Metropolitan or the Louvre, encompassing the visual culture of all humanity, back to the Egyptians and Greeks, out to the Polynesians and Africans, although all four of those particular cultures have been represented in excellent exhibitions in recent years. They are not represented in the permanent collections, which, with an occasional, almost accidental digression, concentrate fairly strictly on the main line of European art from late medieval and early Renaissance through the golden glories of Impressionism and Post-Impressionism, with a smattering of twentieth-century developments in Europe and America. As indicated above, there are two sculpture halls in the West Building, but the overwhelming stress in the collections is on painting in the periods encompassed.

The National is really a collection of collections. It started as the idea of Andrew W. Mellon, the banker, an ambassador and cabinet member for Herbert Hoover. Mellon, involved in a tax trial, offered his collection as the nucleus of a new National Gallery, as well as the building and an endowment, if the government would donate the site and provide all services below the top-management level. The main job of the first two directors was to attract other collections, chiefly those of two individual collectors, two brothers and one father-and-son team. The father and son were Peter A. B. Widener and Joseph E. Widener of Philadelphia, and the collection included decorative arts and a superb collection of Chinese porcelains as well as many of the finest paintings in the Gallery. The two brothers were Samuel and Rush Kress, the chain-store owners, and their collection is the only one the National Gallery's professional staff actually had a hand in forming. Lessing J. Rosenwald, retired chairman of Sears, Roebuck & Co., became a great connoisseur of prints and drawings. His collection has made the National one of the most important centers of graphics, while his rare-book collection has enhanced the Library of Congress. The fifth of the core collections at the Gallery came from Chester Dale, like Mellon a financier. Dale's area of concentration was French Impressionism and Post-Impressionism, with some additions from the twentieth-century successors to those movements and some works by earlier artists felt to be influences on his beloved French painters. Besides these five collections, the National Gallery has accepted donations of individual pictures or smaller groups from many donors and has also been able to buy desired works, privately or at auction, thanks to the financial generosity of the Mellon family and of other benefactors.

Fortunately, the Gallery has been able to strike workable compromises between collectors—most notably, the Wideners—who wanted their collections shown all together, and the sensible universally followed design of Andrew Mellon to group the art by period and by nation; the Italian works are even broken down by city and region.

The visitor can thus arrive in the rotunda, admire Giambologna's *Mercury* and the seasonal floral display if it's the right season, turn to the right, if he has entered from Constitution Avenue, turn right again, and commence a journey through the history and many of the greatest achievements of art from the late Middle Ages to the early twentieth century, simply by following the sequence of galleries from thirteenth-century Florence and Siena to Paris in 1900. Here's the sequence, with a very few of the highlights to watch for:

Tuscan and Umbrian: Giotto and Duccio, of course, with whom it all began; Masaccio, with whom it all began again a hundred years later after things were more or less wiped out by the Black Death; the Fra Angelico/Fra Filippo Lippi collaboration on the *Adoration of the Magi*; Botticelli's *Adoration,* so different, as well as his portrait of his patron, Giuliano de' Medici, and, in a nearby room, Verrocchio's powerful terracotta head of the *capo di tutti capi* in art patronage, Giuliano's brother, Lorenzo the Magnificent; the *Alba Madonna* by Raphael and his youthful *St. George and the Dragon*, and the National's great prize, Leonardo's portrait of Ginevra de' Benci.

North Italian and Venetian: Giorgione, with, probably, an assist from Titian, in *The Adoration of the Shepherds;* Giovanni Bellini's *The Feast of the Gods;* Titian's lush *Venus with A Mirror;* Tintoretto's *Galilee;* and Veronese's extravagant fancy-dress party, *The Finding of Moses.*

Later Italian: Canaletto's view of St. Mark's Square and his view of the Brenta Canal at Padua; Guardi's view of everybody's favorite Venetian ecclesiastical name, the Campo San Zanipolo, with the church of the same name heightened by the addition of a temporary, now long gone, double staircase for the visit of Pope Pius VI; and G.-B. Tiepolo's wonderfully composed and painted *Apollo Pursuing Daphne,* the maiden who turned into a tree rather than submit to divine embraces.

Spanish: The first Spanish gallery adjoins the last Italian ones, the other two are past the German and Low Country rooms for reasons having to do with those original core collections. Herewith the highlights in all three rooms: El Greco's writhing *Laocoon* with its serpentine movements of serpents and people alike; also, that master's *Christ Cleansing the Temple,* the title decorously changed from the traditional *Driving the Money Changers from the Temple;* the wonderfully strong head and shoulders of Pope Innocent X by Velazquez; the same artist's *Needlewoman,* proving as he often did that the lowly and humble could be as interesting to paint as the high and the mighty; Murillo's *Girl and Her Duenna,* a wonderful composition, an even more wonderful double character study; and two magnificent Goya portraits, the Marquesa of Pontejos and Don Bartolome Sureda, which between them, show Goya's best manner with self-infatuated aristocrats and with realistic rising bourgeois.

German: Small or minor pictures by major masters, which still embody the artists' special qualities, include the agonizing *Small Crucifixion* by Mathis Grunewald, the older Cranach's portrait of a woman, a portrait of a clergyman and a remarkably Italianate Madonna and Child by the greatest German, Albrecht Durer, and, in some ways the pride of the group, Hans Holbein's charming portrait of England's Edward VI as a child.

Flemish: Just about every major figure in the golden centuries of Flemish painting is represented. Among them are: Jan Van Eyck in a jewellike *Annunciation,* Petrus Christus in a matched pair of kneeling

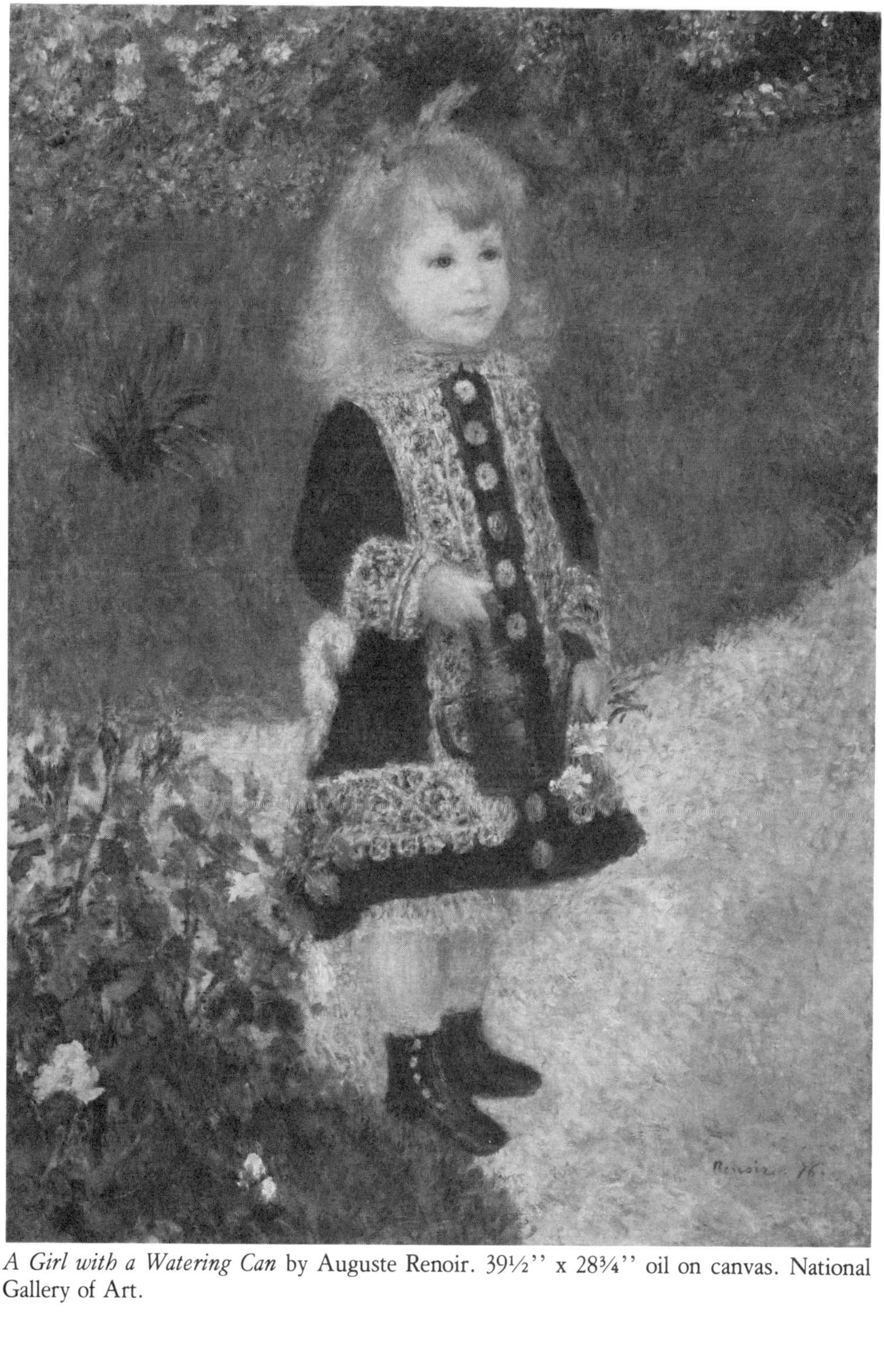

A Girl with a Watering Can by Auguste Renoir. 39½'' x 28¾'' oil on canvas. National Gallery of Art.

donors, man and wife; the mesmerizing portrait of a woman by Rogier van der Weyden; Hans Memling's magical *Presentation in the Temple;* Hieronymous Bosch's *Death and the Miser,* a lesson to us all; the older Breughel's nightmarish *Temptation of St. Anthony;* the glorious Peter Paul Rubens in a poignant portrait of his first wife as she was sickening unto death, and in two painted designs for tapestries—one of which, *The Meeting of Abraham and Melchizedek,* is, among other virtues, a dazzling display of the painter's virtuosity in showing both the scene on the tapestry and the tapestry itself as held by cherubs in the architectural setting it was designed for; and a whole run of portraits by Rubens's favorite pupil and studio assistant, Sir Anthony Van Dyck.

Dutch: The heart of the Dutch section is the extraordinary group of works by Rembrandt, including biblical scenes, portraits, among them the most penetrating self-portrait ever painted, and, in the view of many scholars, the most spiritual landscape ever painted, *The Mill.* Dutch art before Rembrandt is represented by Lucas van Leyden's group of men and women playing cards and arguing over who had or hadn't paid up to the pot, and a splendid group of tough-minded portraits by Frans Hals. The National Gallery has the largest group of Jan Vermeers outside Holland. Special attention should be paid to the picture of the woman weighing gold, full of allegorical meanings, but also full of astonishing sensitivity to light and atmosphere. The "Little Masters," Ter Borch, De Hooch, Cuyp, De Heem, and others are well represented in genre pictures, landscapes, and still lifes. Of special interest is Jacob van Ruisdal's forest scene with rocks, water, and fallen trees.

French, Seventeenth and Eighteenth Centuries: This was the period when primacy in painting, so long held by the Italians, passed to the French, with whom it remained until the mid-twentieth century. The masters who made this possible are all present, from Francois Clouet's portrait of Diane de Poitiers in her bath, through Claude Lorrain, Poussin, and Louis Le Nain, to the rich flowering in Watteau, whose *Italian Comedians* itself symbolizes the passing of cultural leadership from the south to the French, in Boucher's adorable nude Venus, in Fragonard's large, sunlit afternoon games and in his solid, pensive picture of a young girl reading a book, in Chardin's domesticity.

British: Painting in England had traditionally been something imported from the Continent, like wine and music, but in the eighteenth century a native school developed fruitfully, and those masters are all here: the three R's of Reynolds, Romney, and Raeburn in very sensitive portraits; the first flowering of English landscape in Gainsborough, as well as some of his portraits; that quintessential painter of British aristocrats and their horses, George Stubbs, who manages to make the horse the hero of a family group in a landscape; and, the twin summits of British painting, Constable and Turner, the former especially in two absolute masterpieces of light and land, *Wivenhoe Park* and a view of Salisbury Cathedral, the latter especially in a moonlight scene of coal heaving for the new combination of sail-and-steam vessels and in the stormy view of the confluence of the Thames and the Medway.

American: To see American art in historical depth in Washington, it is necessary to go elsewhere, namely the Corcoran, the Phillips, and the National Collection of Fine Arts. But the National does have a choice group of top-flight individual works by individual masters of its own country: a Benjamin West military portrait of a British commander with Indian aide; Copley's portrait of his own family; one of the finest Gilbert Stuarts ever painted, the portrait of Mrs. Yates; Winslow Homer's shot, so to speak, two ducks hit on the wing, Whistler's *White Girl,* a Sargent street scene in Venice; one of the almost miraculous Eakins boat-racing pictures; and the strongest Mary Cassatt painting, *The Boating Party.* In recent years the Gallery has been adding more recent paintings by Abstract Expressionists and others, but in line with standing policy, these have not been given permanent places since the artists are not yet dead twenty years. Some are on view in the East Building.

French Nineteenth Century: Thanks to Chester Dale, this category, a great popular favorite, is second only to Italian art in the space occupied in the Gallery. Everyone you ever heard of in that golden period is present, many of them in absolute masterpieces. Perhaps the all-time favorite is Renoir's child holding a watering-can, a portrait of the painter's son, Jean, later a great film director. Others include Degas dancers, Monet in Venice, Gauguin in the South Seas, Boudin on the Brittainy coast, Pissarro on the boulevards, Van Gogh in the olive orchards of the south, Lautrec in the no-less-steamy dance halls of Paris.

Others: on the ground floor of the West Building may be found the Kress Collection of Renaissance bronzes, mostly medals and medallions, the Widener Chinese porcelains, tapestries, and furnishings, as well as one of the largest and by far the lowest-price shop of art reproductions in the world. Paintings come in sizes from postcards on up to "suitable for framing," in several sizes already suitably framed. The bronzes just mentioned are reproduced as buckles, broaches, cuff links, and earrings.

Activities

Those low-cost reproductions of Gallery works are part of an elaborate education program the National has engaged in from the start. This includes regular tours, the rental of talking guides, the loan of slides and tapes on the collections, and a series of Sunday-afternoon lectures that include the distinguished Bollingen Lectures on art.

Exhibitions

The opening of the East Building in 1978 abruptly launched the National Gallery in a new career as a major creator and exhibitor of special shows, some large and spectacular, others small and intimate. The new building's exhibition rooms are entirely devoted to special shows. Recent ones have included the great Munch, Pacific Island, and Thyssen Collection exhibitions, as well as the American Luminist show and the Post-Impressionist show.

Music

The National Gallery is probably the only art museum in the world with a resident staff conductor and composer who presides over a weekly, Sunday-night concert by a chamber orchestra. The repertoire regularly includes new works by young composers and solo performances by young vocalists and instrumentalists.

Museum of History & Technology

National Museum of History and Technology 14th Street and Constitution Ave. NW 381-6586 Daily: 10-5:30, Summer hours: 10-10 Closed Christmas Day Admission free

The Museum of History and Technology is what people had in mind when they first called the Smithsonian Institution "the nation's attic." The attic has been cleaned up considerably since then. Specifically, the Museum of History and Technology occupies a lovely new building with plenty of space for the exercise of museology on a large scale. At one time, the vast holdings of the Smithsonian were jammed together in no easily discernible order; in the new building every department is laid out so as to make the most visual and intellectual sense to the visitor.

The Collections

The collections are many, and each of them is substantial, as you would expect from a museum with those two far-reaching words in its title. Several, however, are of special interest to art lovers, starting with the Jose Rivera slowly revolving stainless steel sculpture on its plinth facing the Mall.

The Ceramics and Glass Division comes as close to being comprehensive as you can get. The earliest examples of glass on view date from 1500 B.C. There are plenty of samples of European and American glassware from the fourteenth century to the present. Early American glass is well covered, as are the glass objects produced in American furnaces in the late nineteenth and twentieth centuries.

Special strengths are found in the Han Sys Collection of eighteenth-century European porcelain, the Larson Collection of nineteenth-century transfer-printed English earthenware, and the complementary McCauley Collection of Liverpool-type earthenware.

Besides the obvious historical value of such a collection, the importance of such assemblages for the private collector is to allow him to sharpen his or her eye, taste, and knowledge on examples that are completely researched, identified, and, often, exhibited so as to make comparisons easy, both with items of the same general kind and, especially here, with the Oriental wares that were the inspiration of so much European work.

The Graphic Arts Division is focused on printing in all its aspects, which include a generous representation of fine-art printing. We see the tools and effects of the classical processes: woodblock, woodcut, engraving, etching, and lithography, as well as those of later developments. Patent Office models from the exploding technology of printing in the second half of the nineteenth century illustrate the changing and proliferating methods of printmaking and of printing. In addition to this basic teaching role, the Division regularly mounts special exhibitions of Old Master and more recent prints from its own extensive holdings. Again, as with the glass and ceramics, these shows give the visitor a chance to sharpen his own eye and, of course, to understand the complex processes behind prints.

The Division has moved naturally from the technical processes of printing to the most widely known results of printing, news reporting, and a lively history of the development of that profession enhances the hall.

Related to both printing and news reporting is the Photographic History Division. For the art lover, the heart of this section of the museum will naturally be the masterworks by great photographers to be found among the 50,000 or so photographs the Division owns. Some of these are always on view, but the stress, correctly, is on the history and technology of photographs rather than on the works of art produced in the field.

This is one of the liveliest exhibitions in the whole museum. The visitor gets to experience various forms of past photography, including early stereographs and even earlier fabrications of motion pictures. There is a Trans-Lux newsreel theater in which newsreels of historic people and events run more or less continuously, a re-created parlor scene of a Victorian evening with stereography, the early Eastman photo-finishing operation, early war photographers, and others. Over all the sense of hustle and bustle, however, are those great pictures by master photographers setting the standards for the art that still obtain.

Transportaion

The National Museum of History and Technology is handy to two Metro subway stations, Federal Triangle and Smithsonian. It is also served by the red double-decker London bus that shuttles from here to the National Portrait Gallery and back.

Portrait Gallery

National Portrait Gallery F St. at Eighth St. NW 381-5380 Daily: 10-5:30 Closed Christmas Day Admission free

The idea of a National Portrait Gallery is about as old as the Republic, but although there were noble efforts by artists like the Peales and G. P. A. Healy and by collectors and public benefactors like the National Gallery of Art founder Andrew W. Mellon, the Portrait Gallery did not come into existence until 1962, as part of a rescue operation to save the Old Patent Office Building from being sacrificed to the then-insatiable demands for ever more parking space in the District of Columbia.

The Building

The Portrait Gallery occupies, roughly, the south half of what was built as the Patent Office Building, intended to display the fruits of American ingenuity and invention. Since those traits were early regarded as the American equivalent of literary and artistic accomplishment in older cultures, the building was modeled on the Parthenon of Athens. By definition it is noble of proportion. Many details cry out for slow and careful examination, such as the staircases in almost every instance, the suspended balconies in the library, the load-bearing pillars that lighten from floor to floor. If there were nothing in the building at all, it would be well worth a visit for such an ambitious and successful elaboration of masonry architecture just before cast iron began the process of making all this obsolete.

The Collection

The heart of the collection is the run of presidents' portraits that presents the faces of our chief executives from Washington on as they were seen by competent, if not always first-rank, portrait artists of their day. The

Lansdowne portrait of Washington by Gilbert Stuart is a noble work, a full-length standing figure making a completely believable gesture of noble presentation or acceptance of homage that became increasingly difficult for both portraitists and presidents to perform as the history of the Republic proceeded. In contrast, Eisenhower, by Thomas E. Stephens, just sits there, hat in hand, coat over arm, as if patiently prepared to depart, awaiting the signal. Other faces in the crowd include those of actors, entertainers, writers, politicians, liberationists—everyone, ideally, who made some significant contribution to the evolution of the Republic or to the American people. The Healy portraits of presidents form one core group in the collection, the St. Memin heads and busts of "the first families in America," form another, and a third is the portrait group acquired by Andrew W. Mellon specifically for a portrait gallery when one should come into being.

Exhibitions

Within the narrow boundaries of its concerns, the Portrait Gallery manages to be quite extensive in its special exhibition program. Recent shows have included the war works of Howard Chandler Christy, with their fascinating combination of World War I patriotism and sex appeal, and the characters and causes of the famed "Monkey Trial," which pitted William Jennings Bryan against Clarence Darrow.

Tours

Tours can be scheduled for groups or individuals seven days a week between 10 and 3. Call 381-6347.

Transportation

The National Portrait Gallery is convenient to the Gallery Place station of the Metro subway system. It is also served by a free double-decker bus from—and back to—the Museum of History and Technology on the Mall.

Organization of American States

Organization of American States 17th St. at Constitution Ave. NW
and The Museum of Modern Art of Latin America 201 18th St. NW
Tuesday-Saturday: 10-5 Closed Sunday, Monday, and holidays
Admission free

The Organization of American States, previously known as the Pan American Union, is the treaty group of the states of the Western Hemisphere—North, South, and Central America. The original building, still referred to by Washingtonians as the Pan American Union, was designed for the meetings of the representatives of the republics and the housing of the staff necessary to keep the organization going. For many years and continuing today, the OAS has held regular, changing art exhibitions in the main building. These are usually one-artist shows, and while there is no regular rotation among the republics, over the course of a couple of years, most of the Spanish- or Portuguese-speaking nations are represented in the program. Canadian representation is much rarer and that of United States artists almost unknown. One result of this is that Latin American art is much more familiar to Washington art lovers than it is to most other Americans. Also, Washington collectors tend to collect Latin American art more than their counterparts elsewhere in the country.

The Building

The original building, on 17th St., is beaux-arts in architecture applied to a South American hacienda with Pre-Columbian details—a relatively rare bird in Washington—and the combination is fascinating. The facade, and still more the interior court, which the visitor crosses to see the temporary exhibitions, is a kind of solid embodiment of the Spanish dreams of MGM in its classical period.

The building behind this *estancia* was originally made to provide a courtyard complementary facade. It still does that, but the effect is no longer regularly visible. Instead, the visitor enters from 18th St. and never gets to see that facing facade at all. The compensation is the Museum of Modern Art of Latin America.

The Collection As part of the hemispheric celebration of the 200th anniversary of American Independence, the OAS dedicated this building to a permanent collection of modern Latin American art. Obviously, such a field, to be comprehensive, would take many times the space of this essentially residential-size building. On two floors, the museum shows examples of the best-known twentieth-century artists from south of the Rio Grande, interspersed with paintings and sculptures by Latin artists not so well known. Many if not all of the best-known names are present: Candido Portinari, Torres-Garcia, Penalba, Orozco, Tamayo, Matta, Cuevas, Obregon, Mabe, Carlos Merida, Jesus Soto.

Going through the collection, the visitor usually comes to some vague understanding of a common note, or a group of common notes, to be found in much Latin American art regardless of formal differences. There is, often at least, a feeling of bright light in the midst of surrounding darkness, whether the subject is a group of dancers in some public room, the cubistically rendered forms of a wake for a dead man, or a geometric structure relating to nothing but geometry. The precise formulation of such a definition or description of Latin art is best left to the individual visitor.

The Phillips

The Phillips Collection 1600-1612 21st. St. NW 387-2151 Tuesday-Saturday: 10-5, Sunday: 2-7 Closed Mondays, New Year's Day, the Fourth of July, Thanksgiving, and Christmas Admission free

The Phillips is the oldest museum of modern art in the country, if not the world. Founded in 1918 by Duncan Phillips as a memorial to his father and brother, the Collection is thus a good decade older than the Museum of Modern Art in New York. From the first, the Phillips has a propagandizing intent on behalf of the acceptance of modern art, but the propaganda was the gentlest—and most effective—kind, merely the presentation of the opportunity to see examples. At first intensely American, perhaps in response to the patriotism engendered by World War I, the Collection, along with its founders and directors, Duncan and Marjorie Phillips, soon opened its eyes to the achievements of twentieth-century European modernism. The Phillipses hung their pictures in their house, a fine old 1890s brownstone, eventually moved out, leaving the building to be all museum, and finally built an annex. The feeling of being in someone's home has never been lost and is a great part of the charm the Phillips exerts on all who know it. The new wing preserves

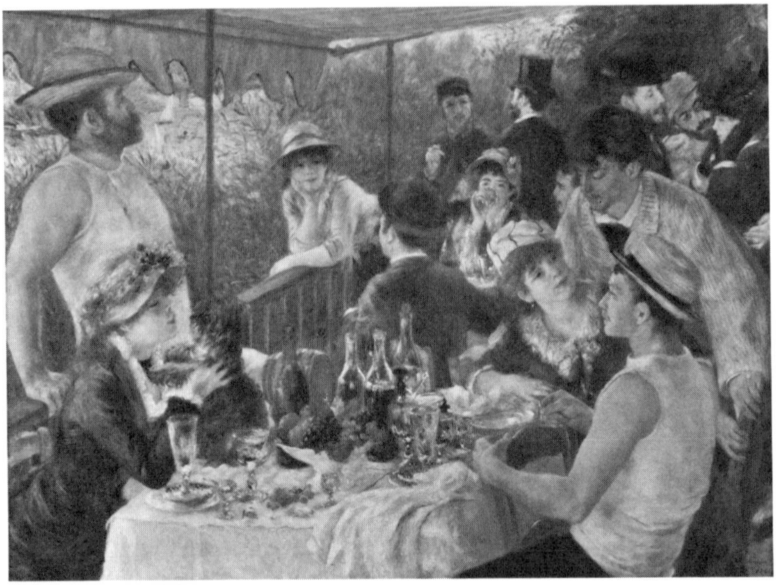

Luncheon of the Boating Party by Auguste Renoir. 51'' x 68'' oil on canvas. The Phillips Collection.

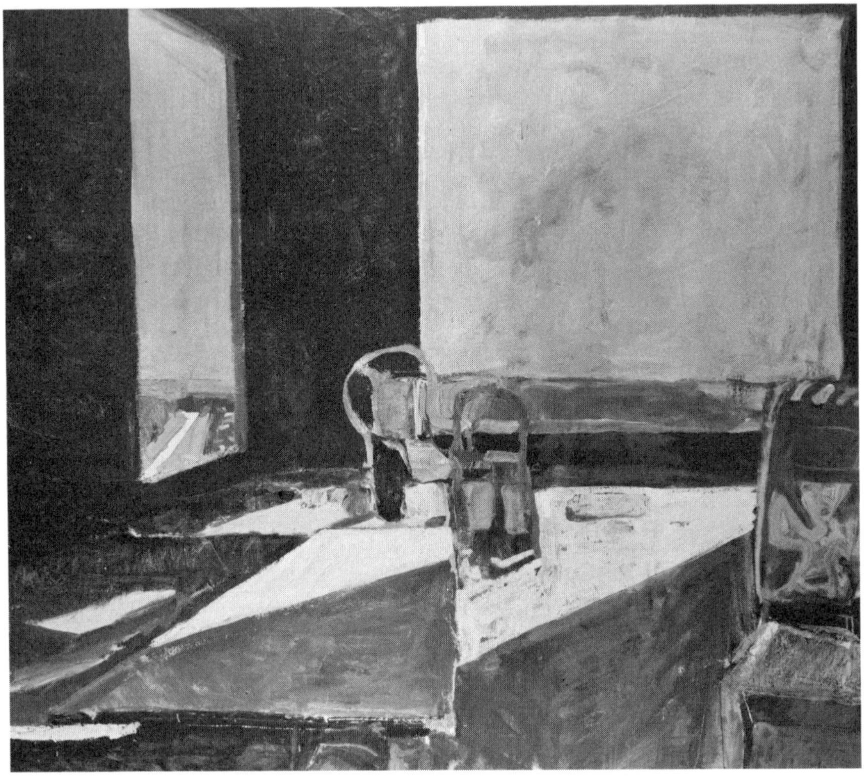

Interior with View of the Ocean by Richard Diebenkorn. 49 5/8'' x 57 3/4'' oil on canvas. The Phillips Collection.

that feeling with carpets, comfortable chairs, and sofas, even an occasional window.

The Collection The Collection has been shaped by two very conscious plans made by Mr. and Mrs. Phillips. The first was that it was to be "a museum of modern art and its sources." They never did define "sources" too closely, and as a happy result, the Collection includes some great older works, most notably the pair of paintings of *The Repentant Peter* by the two Spanish masters, centuries apart, El Greco and Goya; the magnificent Eakins portrait of *Miss Van Buren;* a tiny, rainbowlike landscape by Giorgione, or, as the Phillips has always labeled it, "Giorgione (?)," and pictures by Constable and Chardin, Ingres and Delacroix, among others.

The second guiding principle of the Phillipses was set by their evangelism for art. They built what Duncan called "units" of the work of particularly favorite artists, or of artists they regarded as of special significance. When it was possible, they bought a number of paintings of such artists. Due to the early pro-Americanism of the Collection, it is very strong in such pioneer American modernists as Georgia O'Keeffe, John Marin, Arthur Dove, the American inventor of nonobjective art, and Karl Knaths, who headed the art school in the years when that was part of the museum. Augustus Tack, another American early nonobjective painter, is better represented at the Phillips than at any other museum. Outstanding among the Europeans with strong "units" of their own are Georges Braque, Paul Klee, Edouard Vuillard, Pierre Bonnard, Georges Rouault, Oscar Kokoschka, and Nicholas de Stael.

By far the best-known single painting in the Phillips is the best Renoir that master ever painted, arguable the best Impressionist picture, *The Luncheon of the Boating Party.* Now hung in the new wing in a small gallery it easily dominates, the *Boating Party* repays the lengthy study the setting makes easy. It contains brilliant still-life painting, figure groups, portraits, even touches of both landscape and anecdote all brought together in a glorious Impressionist celebration of light.

The small gallery holding the Collection's Rothkos is by far the most effective exhibition of his quiet, luminous paintings to be found anywhere. For the solitary visitor—and the Phillips is the kind of place where you can be a solitary visitor—the paintings do what they're supposed to do, invite your own projections on their gently glowing, colored screens.

Often hung together, the Rouaults and the Monticellis reveal unexpected affinities, which indeed has always been one of the great virtues of the Phillips. The little room housing the little paintings of Paul Klee is quite magical, tiny window after tiny window opening on a world quite unlike the one we know, yet one we feel we can understand and like. In total contrast the great city-landscapes of Kokoschka, also often hung together, reveal familiar kinds of city scenes suddenly in all-new perspective. The flower paintings, landscapes, and one surprising night-baseball scene by cofounder Marjorie Phillips offer clues as to what else is in store. Such are a few of the joys of the Phillips Collection.

Exhibitions With very rare exceptions, the exhbitions at the Phillips tend to be one-man shows. The range is from old masters of the modern school to young artists you may not have heard of. In celebration of the Bicentennial, the Collection devoted most of its 1976 schedule to an all but exhaustive series of exhibitions of its own holdings in American art, naturally strongly tilted toward the twentieth century, though with a rich background of the nineteenth. That was an extraordinarily useful series of shows, and happily it has left a permanent effect. The visitor sees more early American moderns than used to be visible.

Programs The Phillips has been perhaps the single most effective force for modern music in Washington, as it has been for modern art in America. Concerts are presented September through May every Sunday except Easter at 5 P.M. Admission is free, early arrival advised, and you are more likely than not to hear at least one composer or performer unfamiliar yet of obvious interest.

Transportation From the Federal-museum area of the District of Columbia, where most visitors spend most of their time, take the Metro Red Line to the Dupont Circle station, walk west on Massachusetts Avenue for the few blocks to 21st St. The Phillips will be on your right.

Renwick

Renwick Gallery of The National Collection of Fine Arts Pennsylvania Ave. at 17th St. NW 381-5811 Daily: 10-5:30 Closed Christmas Day Admission free

Housed in the oldest operating museum building in Washington, the Renwick is among the youngest museums. It is also a museum with a split personality. The building was erected in 1859 by Washington collector and founder of the gallery that bears his name, William W. Corcoran, to show his collection to the public. The Civil War postponed his plans. The building served as a storehouse and headquarters of the Union Quartermaster-General, not opening as a museum until 1874. When the Corcoran moved to its present building, a few blocks down 17th St., at the turn of the century, this building once more reverted to government use as the U.S. Court of Claims. Threatened with destruction in the 1960s, it was saved for the NCFA and made into the institution it now is.

The split personality comes from its two totally unrelated purposes: in the Grand Salon and the Octagon Room on the second floor, the Renwick re-creates the Corcoran Collection as it looked, more or less, in Mr. Corcoran's day: rather uninspiring pictures hung in tiers on the walls, elaborate furnishings, some nice porcelain and bric-a-brac; on the ground floor and elsewhere on the second, the Renwick conducts one of the liveliest, most stimulating changing exhibition programs in crafts and design to be found anywhere in the world.

The Building The building itself is a splendid example of nineteenth-century grandeur at its grandest, with domes, arches, architraves, pediments, niches, medallions, and other decorative embellishments. The Grand Salon is the Gilded Age, the pictures the taste of the time. The whole is a kind of time capsule, worth more in its over-all effect than in all of the individual parts. Most visitors will never have heard of most of the artists

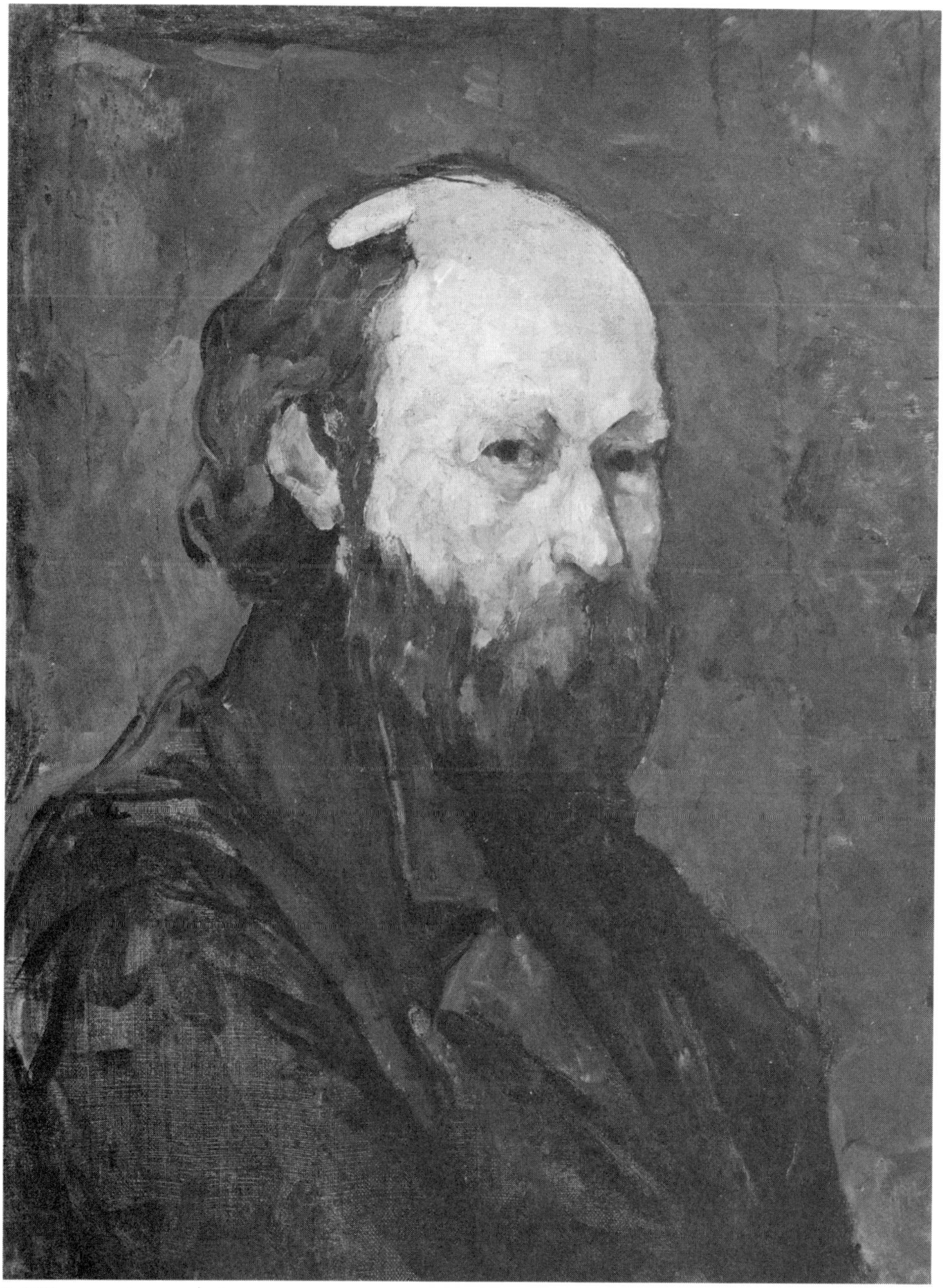

Self Portrait by Paul Cezanne. 24'' x 18½'' oil on canvas. The Phillips Collection.

represented, but it was they—not their contemporaries, Corot, Courbet, Manet, Monet, and the rest—who actually dominated established art in the period.

Exhibitions The craft and design exhibition program is an unending source of revelation, even to those who think they know those fields fairly well. The main focus is on American designers and craftsmen, but occasionally the work of other people is shown. Recent exhibitions include a survey of the past century of ceramics in the United States, a broad survey of worldwide glassmaking now, an assemblage of American Indian tipi designs, and a look at pop-commercial signs and designs for gas stations, fast-food outlets, and things of that ilk. Always stimulating, always instructive, the Renwick is a rewarding place to visit.

The Renwick is named for its architect, James Renwick, who also designed the "Castle," the Smithsonian's headquarters on the Mall, and St. Patrick's Cathedral, New York.

Tours Guided tours are conducted weekdays at 10, 11, and 1 by appointment only. 381-6541.

Transportation Renwick Gallery is across Pennsylvania Avenue from the Executive Office Building just west of the White House and is near the Farragut West station on the Metro subway system.

Textile

The Textile Museum 2320 S St. NW 667-0441 Tuesday-Saturday: 10-5 Closed Sunday, Monday, and national holidays Admission free, contribution suggested: Adults $1, Children 50c

Like the Phillips Collection a few blocks away, the Textile Museum is essentially the product of one very zealous collector and is housed in what was his own home. The man was George Hewitt Myers, as in Bristol-Myers. He began buying rugs while a sophomore at Yale in the 1890s just to have something to put on the floor of his room. One rug led to another, and by the time he founded the museum in 1925, he had thousands and he and his wife were still actively buying. The result is a collection of rugs and other textiles that has only one rival in the country—the department at the Metropolitan Museum of Art, New York.

The Building The principal building is not all that distinguished, but it was the work of a favorite, domesticated in every sense, self-taught architect of the region, Waddy Wood, who built the Woodrow Wilson House next door. The house on the other side, where the Myers actually lived, was the work of John Russell Pope and is more elegant in every way. Taken together, the three represent a local variation in what may have been the most comfortable and commodious home-building this country ever knew.

The Collection The principal area of concentration for Mr. Myers and his museum has been the whole, vast "rug culture," which takes in all of North Africa, the Arabian peninsula, Turkey, the Caucausus, India, Tibet, China, Korea, and Japan, to name only the most prominent producers of textiles. For Mr. Myers, the drive was always to what came before the rug he had just purchased, and thus the collection is remarkable for linkages and relationships.

Besides the rugs there are very rare ancient garments and cloth from Pre-Columbian Peru as well as some of the knotted strings by which the Incas communicated along their high highways. But the rugs are the main attraction. The somewhat out of the way location should not discourage anyone who really cares about rugs, and a visit here can gradually teach the uninstructed visitor to distinguish among the hundreds of different patterns and weaves.

Exhibitions

In addition to putting on exhibitions of private collections and of the museum's own holdings in specified areas, the Textile Museum involves itself in strictly contemporary textile work of all kinds and from all countries, presenting such work in one-artist or group exhibitions. The Textile also has one of the most interesting museum shops in Washington, offering materials and patterns for the ambitious textile worker as well as exotic ceramics, printed textiles, and jewelry brought back by the trustees from their own travels in the rug lands.

Transportation

Taxi or private car provide the easiest ways to get to the museum from almost anywhere. On the other hand, in fine weather it is a pleasant walk from Dupont Circle Metro subway station on the Red Line and half that distance from the Phillips Collection.

The Galleries

Gallery Specializations

Many of the galleries found below exhibit a wide variety of art styles and mediums. The following list represents concentrations of a particular artistic mode rather than the individual focus of the gallery. Thus, some galleries that exhibit many styles may be found in several listings. Some, but not all, of the galleries which are listed under a specialization are classified on the basis of excellence in that respective area, rather than for the size of their collections.

American Contemporary — Bader, Baumgartner, Brown, Capricorn, Fendrick, Fiedler, Fondo del Sol, Foundry, Gallery 4, Gallery K, Gallery 10, Govinda, Hallway, Haslem, Henri, Hull, I.F.A., Local 1734, Lunn, McIntosh/Drysdale, Mickelson, Middendorf/Lane, Miya, Osuna, Paul VI, Plum, Premiere, Rasmussen, Spectrum, Studio, Torpedo Factory, Touchstone, Via Gambaro, Washington Women's Arts Center, Washington World, Zenith.

American Periods — Adams Davidson, Atlantic, Atlantic Gallery Graphics, Bethesda Art Gallery, Capricorn, Graphic Antiquity, Haslem, Hom, Hull, Kathleen Ewing, Middendorf/Lane, Montrose, Old Print Gallery, Pensler, Tolley.

European & Other Continents: Contemporary — Amerasia, Atlantic, Old Warsaw, Osuna, Shogun, Venable-Neslage.

European & Other Continents: Periods — Shogun, Veerhoff.

Primitive/Ancient — Trocadero, Volta Place.

Crafts — Branch, Fendrick, Glass Gallery, Greenwood, Paul VI, Plum, Seraph, Touchstone, Via Gambaro, Zenith.

Washington Art Coops — Local 1734, Miya, Spectrum, Studio, Touchstone, Washington Women's Arts Center.

Graphics Contemporary — Franz Bader, Baumgartner, Capitol East, Capricorn, Fendrick, Fiedler, Gage, Gallery 4, Gallery 10, Hallway, Haslem, Hull, I.F.A., Local 1734, Mickelson, Middendorf/Lane, Old Warsaw, Plum, Premiere, Paul Rosen, Shogun, Torpedo Factory, Touchstone, Venable-Neslage.

Graphics Period — Atlantic Gallery Graphics, Bethesda Art Gallery, Capricorn, Haslem, Hom, Mickelson, Shogun.

Photography Contemporary — Ewing, Intuitiveye, Lunn, Sander, Washington Women's Arts Center, Woodfin Camp.

Photography Vintage — Ewing, Graphic Antiquity, Lunn, Sander.

Sculpture — Bader, Brown, Fiedler, Fondo del Sol, Gallery 10, Henri, Hom, McIntosh/Drysdale, Mickelson, Middendorf/Lane, Osuna, Rasmussen, Studio, Tolley, Touchstone, Zenith.

The Galleries by locations

Adams Morgan
Middendorf/Lane Gallery

Capitol Hill
Capitol East Graphics
Via Gambaro Gallery

Downtown
Franz Bader Gallery
Diane Brown Gallery
Gallery Amerasia
Intuitiveye Gallery
Lunn Gallery
McIntosh/Drysdale Gallery
Mickelson Gallery
Miya Gallery
Osuna Gallery
Jack Rasmussen Gallery
Studio Gallery
Tolley Galleries
WPA (Washington Project for the Arts)
Woodfin Camp Inc.

Dupont Circle
Baumgartner Galleries
Barbara Fiedler Gallery
Fondo del Sol Gallery
Foundry Gallery
Gallery K
Gallery 10
Georgetown Art Gallery
Greenwood Gallery
Jane Haslem Gallery
Henri Gallery
Hom Gallery
Local 1734 Art Collective
Touchstone Gallery
Trocadero Arts of Asia
Veerhoff Gallery
Venable Neslage Galleries
Washington Women's Arts Center
Zenith Gallery

Georgetown
Adams Davidson Galleries
Atlantic Gallery
Atlantic Gallery Graphics
Branch Gallery
Kathleen Ewing Gallery
Fendrick Gallery
Gage Gallery
Govinda Gallery
Graphic Antiquity
Hallway Gallery
Old Print Gallery
Pensler Galleries
Paul Rosen Graphics Ltd.
Seraph Gallery
Shogun Gallery
Spectrum Gallery
Volta Place Gallery
Washington World Gallery

Maryland
Bethesda Art Gallery
Capricorn Galleries
Gallery H
Glass Gallery of Eveleth & Summerford
Montrose Galleries
Paul VI Gallery
Plum Gallery
Premiere Galerie

Old Town/Alexandria
Gallery 4
Old Warsaw Galleries, Inc.
Torpedo Factory

Uptown/D.C.
Art Barn
Hull Gallery
I.F.A. Galleries
Sander Gallery

The Galleries

Adams Davidson

Adams Davidson Galleries 3233 P St. NW 965-3800 Tuesday-Friday: 10-5 Saturday: 12-6

While most commercial galleries in Washington deal in contemporary art, Adams Davidson, since 1965, has steadfastly represented the nineteenth- and early-twentieth-centuries, from the Hudson River School through American Impressionism and "The Eight." The recent revival of interest in this field, and the subsequent boom in this market, has turned this rather sedate, former three-story Georgetown house into a mecca for serious collectors and investors. If proprietor Ted Cooper is not on hand, he is likely to be shuttling around the country in search of paintings to buy. Selling them, he maintains, is no longer a problem.

Cooper, an art historian, deals with big names when he can get them, often in the form of smaller paintings, watercolors, and drawings which he shows in six well-documented group exhibitions each year. Each has its own illustrated catalog to accommodate an out-of-town clientele. "Works on Paper," for example, might feature no lesser lights than Rembrandt Peale, Thomas Cole, Frederic Church, Thomas Eakins, Winslow Homer, Childe Hassam, Robert Henri, and Maurice Prendergast, among others. When the National Gallery organized its "American Light" show in 1980, which surveyed a group of long-neglected American landscape painters called "Luminists," Cooper was ready with a gallery full of works by many of the artists in that exhibition, among them Sanford Gifford, Martin Johnson Heade, John Frederick Kensett, Alfred Thompson Bricher, Albert Bierstadt, Jasper Cropsey, William Trost Richards, John Henry Hill, and Fitz Hugh Lane.

Though the gallery does not show work by living artists on a regular basis, Cooper's bias toward traditional realism makes this the most likely place to find resales of the occasional drawings or paintings by N. C. Wyeth, Andrew Wyeth, and Jamie Wyeth that do turn up. European Old Masters, too, can often be found perched against the wall in a special viewing room on the third floor. Cooper has also qualified as a member of the American Society of Appraisers.

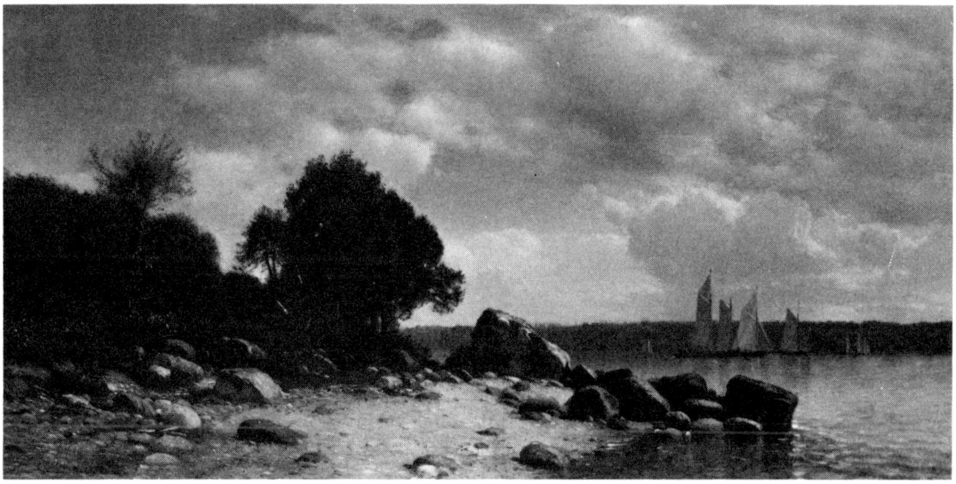

Hudson River Landscape by Samuel Coleman. 15'' x 30'' oil on canvas. Adams Davidson Gallery.

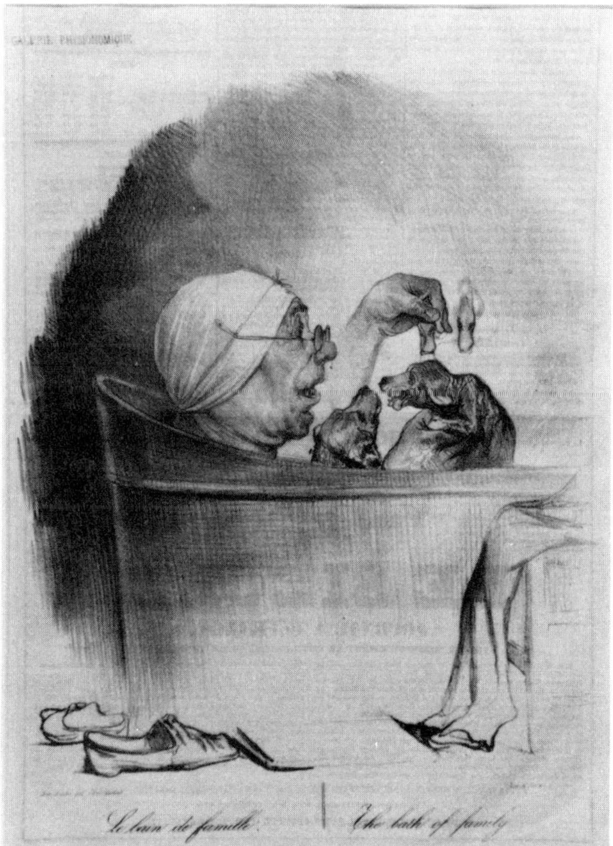

Le Bain de Famille by Honore Daumier. 9¾'' x 14'' lithograph. Atlantic Gallery Graphics.

Amerasia Gallery Amerasia 2142 F St. NW 331-0129 Monday-Friday: 9-5

The arrival of Gallery Amerasia in 1976 marked the growth of an ethnic component in the Washington art scene. Focusing on Asian-style art made in America, this gallery is sponsored by the nonprofit Asian Benevolent Corps, and aims to help give talented, professional Asian-American artists living in the metropolitan area a place to show. The charming genre scenes of Shien-ming Yang, landscapes and flowers by Alfred Liu and Helen Mai-Shih McCarthy, silkscreen prints by Peggy Zee, and photographs of Noel Izon are works of artists who are highly accomplished. American artists who do Asian-style work, such as calligraphy, are also shown here.

The gallery also brings special exhibitions from Asia to Washington. "Ten Peking Artists" and "Korean Folk Art" were recent examples. Gallery Amerasia is located near the campus of George Washington University.

Art Barn The Art Barn 2401 Tilden St. NW 426-6719 Wednesday-Sunday: 10-5

A non-profit, community-oriented gallery, the Art Barn is devoted to showing work by groups of area artists not often seen elsewhere. Recent examples include a show by the Korean Artists' Association and "Diplomats in the Arts."

Located in a rustic old mill in the middle of Rock Creek Park, the Art Barn tends to breadth rather than quality, though good shows do occur. They change monthly, and works are usually for sale.

The sylvan setting makes a visit worthwhile, especially on a hot day. Special free arts and crafts demonstrations often take place on weekends.

Atlantic Atlantic Gallery 1055 Thomas Jefferson St. NW 337-2299 Monday-Saturday: 10-6 Thursday: 10-9 Sunday: 1-5

After three years, this Georgetown gallery, located in the new Foundry Building complex on the C & O Canal, continues to specialize in marine and landscape paintings and hunting scenes by nineteenth-century British artists, along with a growing sub-specialty in American art of the period.

The gallery also does a brisk business in the work of John Stobart, a contemporary American marine artist who does paintings of Georgetown and nearby Alexandria, Virginia, as they looked in the 1840s. The paintings rarely come on the market here, though photo-reproductions of them—issued in signed, "limited" editions of 750 each—are sold here for between $200 and $600 each. The gallery, similarly, sells both original paintings and prints and photo-reproductions of work by Pat Buckley Moss, who does quaint scenes of Mennonite life. A whole gallery is devoted to her work, which the gallery publishes.

Among the more interesting original works of art are a small group of British watercolors dating from between 1780 and 1850 by John Clevely, Samuel Atkins, Dominic Serres, and William Joy, all part of the stock owner Malcolm Henderson brought with him from his former gallery in London. The nineteenth-century American art is limited, but has included works by Alfred Thompson Bricher, John Kensett, and marine painters James Buttersworth, William Edward Norton, and Frederick Waugh. There are also some extraordinary original watercolors of birds by the contemporary Australian artist Robin Hill.

Atlantic Graphics

Atlantic Gallery Graphics 1058 Thomas Jefferson St. NW 333-1040
Tuesday-Saturday: 11-5 Sunday: 1-5

British etchings dating from 1900 to 1928—the heyday of British etching—are the featured items here. There are landscapes, figures, and many marine scenes, a holdover from the days when the gallery was owned by Atlantic Gallery, just across the street. People who love boats and the sea (and good art) may well be able to find a nice little print here by English etcher Nelson Dawson, Arthur Briscoe, or W. L. Wyllie and at modest prices.

There are also some drypoints of London and New York by William Walcot, architectural etchings by D. Y. Cameron, and, moving on to Paris, some Daumier lithographs from ''Charivari.'' There are portraits by Swedish artist Anders Zorn and a few scattered examples by Americans Joseph Pennell, James McNeill Whistler, and Gerald Brockhurst.

The stock is mixed, and includes reproductions of old prints, along with some purely decorative contemporary work. But there are enough good things to make a visit worthwhile for print-lovers.

Bader

Franz Bader Gallery 2001 I St. NW 337-5440 Tuesday-Saturday: 10-6

Since 1939, when he left his Vienna bookshop just ahead of the Nazis, Franz Bader has become a legendary figure in Washington as proprietor of the city's longest-running commercial gallery. It is still one of the best, and, happily, the old-world charm has not been lost in a recent move to expanded quarters on the ground floor of an undistinguished office building just one block off Pennsylvania Avenue. Bader's fine bookshop, devoted to the best art publications from all over the world, still occupies a cozy and inviting space at the front of the gallery.

Bader began his career with big-name Europeans, but soon began championing the growing band of painters and sculptors who were working in Washington after World War II, among them Sarah Baker, Ben Summerford, and Leonard Maurer of American University, and Pietro Lazzari, Mitchell Jamieson, color painter Alma Thomas, and more. Watercolorist Lee Weiss and famed printmaker Peter Milton had their first shows with Bader and continue to show there, though they have moved elsewhere. Anita Bucherer from Germany and Dutch painters Henri Plaat and Pim Leefsma are also gallery regulars.

Among many distinguished printmakers who also show regularly are the great Japanese woodblock artist Un'Ichi Hiratsuka, who has been declared a "National Treasure" by the government of Japan, and Prentiss Taylor, Naul Ojeda, Robert Nelson, David Freed, and Mark Leithauser, whose meticulous landscape etchings are eagerly collected here.

Other gallery artists include Herman Maril, Alfred McAdams, Arthur Hall Smith and Mildred Thompson, Robert Marx, and whimsical sculptors Berthold Schmutzhart and Mike Auld. Bader also shows Eskimo carvings of the highest quality.

Baumgartner

Baumgartner Galleries 2016 R St. NW 232-6320 Tuesday-Saturday: 11-6 Closed last two weeks in August

After a decade in the area as a private agent for the eccentric Austrian artist Friedensreich Hundertwasser, Manfred Baumgartner, also Austrian-born, has now opened a handsome gallery in a town house just a few blocks from the Phillips Collection. Hundertwasser continues to be the gallery's star, along with a group of Viennese artists who comprise a school of fantastic realism currently centered at the Vienna Academy. Arik Brauer is the best-known in this group.

Since the gallery opened, however, Baumgartner has aggressively sought and promoted a small group of Washington artists whom he now represents both in this country and abroad, notably neopointillist landscape painter Robert Stark, Lucy Clark, and new realist Sherry Kasten. During the gallery's monthly changing shows, other international artists, not previously seen here, have been introduced, among them Japanese watercolorist Yoshi Takahashi, "Dado," a Yugoslav surrealist living in Paris, and Austrian photorealist Gottfried Helnwein.

Bethesda

Bethesda Art Gallery 7950 Norfolk Ave., Bethesda, Maryland 656-6665 Wednesday-Saturday: 11-5 Thursday: 11-8 Closed August

Though located in suburban Bethesda (off Wisconsin Ave. near Old Georgetown Road) this tiny gallery is a must for lovers of early-twentieth-century American prints, in which it deals exclusively. A good stock of etchings and lithographs by the greats of the period, such as George Bellows, John Sloan, Thomas Hart Benton, Raphael Soyer, John Stuart Curry, Walt Kuhn, Louis Lozowick, Martin Lewis, and Howard Cook—along with wood engravings by Rockwell Kent—is always on hand, along with lesser-knowns from the period. Most works are black and white.

Prices are always fair, information correct, mats acid-free, and prints well-documented by the well-informed owner Betty Duffy, who welcomes all comers, be they experts or novices. Since it opened its doors in 1975, Duffy has transformed her gallery into one of Washington's most highly respected establishments, at the same time turning loose a whole new crop of American print addicts.

Monthly shows are always instructive, and often introduce lesser-known aspects of the period, such as "Prints from the World's Fair of

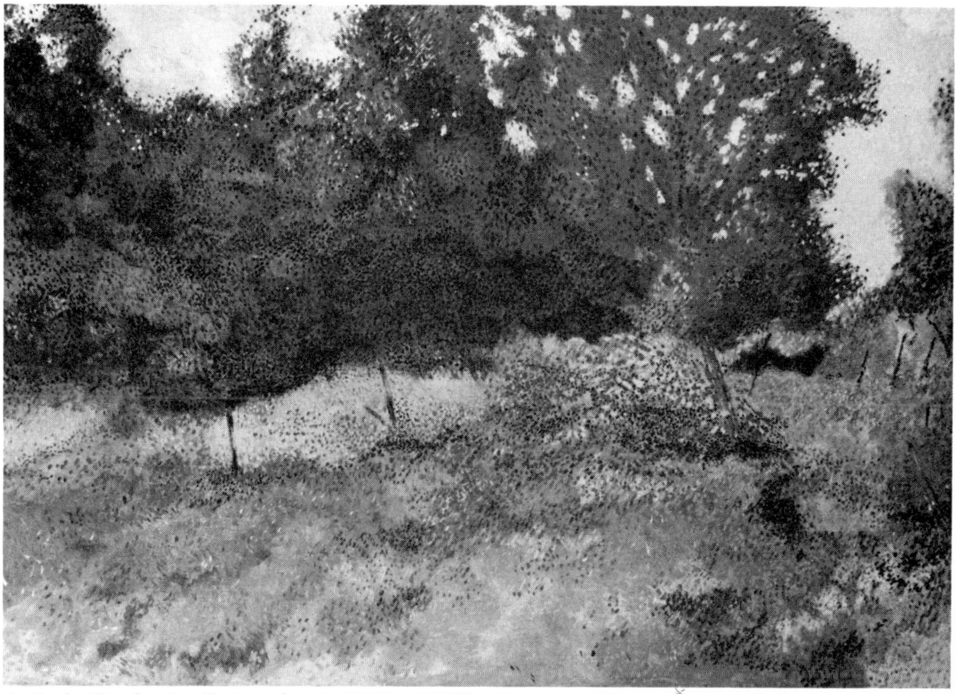

Artist's Garden by Robert Stark. 36'' x 153'' oil on jute. Baumgartner Galleries.

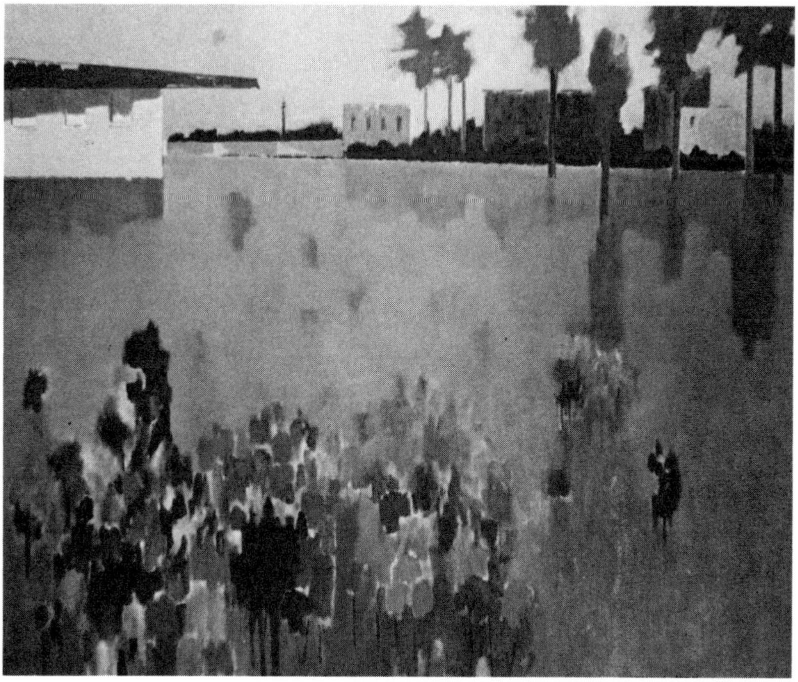

Penney's Garden by Herman Maril. 36'' x 48'' oil on canvas. Franz Bader.

1939," "Early American Silkscreens from the WPA" (where the first American fine-art silkscreens were made), and "Women Printmakers from the 20's, 30's, and 40's," featuring Isabel Bishop, the late Washington caricaturist Aline Fruhauf, Peggy Bacon, and Marguerite Kumm, who still makes delightful miniatures focusing on the artist's life in Washington. Jonathan Meader is among the small group of contemporaries the gallery keeps on hand.

Branch

Branch Gallery 1063 Wisconsin Ave. NW 337-4600 Monday-Thursday: 10-6 Friday-Saturday: 10-midnight Sunday: 1-5

This new gallery is devoted entirely to recent American work in art glass, both blown and sculptural. All pieces are one-of-a-kind and non-utilitarian. The gallery will feature one- and two-person shows each month by 30 artists, known and unknown, now working in this increasingly popular medium. At the rear, representative work by the following artists will ber permanently on view: Michael Cohn, Dale Chihuly, Jon Kuhn, Marvin Lipofsky, Richard Marquis, William Morris, Tom McGlaughlin, Joyce Roessler, Paul Seide, and Ann Warff.

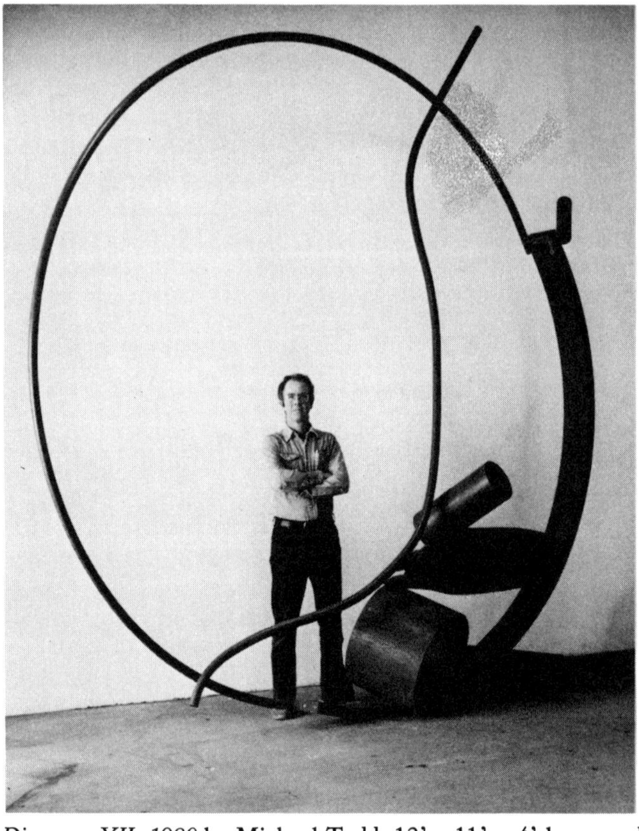

Diamaru XII, 1980 by Michael Todd. 12' x 11' x 4' lacquered steel. Diane Brown.

Brown Diane Brown Gallery 406 Seventh St. NW 296-4022 Tuesday-Saturday: 11-6

After only four years in business, Diane Brown has established herself as one of Washington's leading dealers, particularly in the field of advanced contemporary sculpture from Washington, New York, California, and abroad. The need to show larger works, and more of them, led to the 1979 opening of an auxiliary "Sculpture Space" at 52 O St. NW, a handsome, loft-like area in a former warehouse which also houses several artists' studios. Despite its somewhat remote location, "Sculpture Space" is a must for anyone who has visited the main gallery and wants to see more. It is open Friday and Saturday, noon to 6, and by appointment.

Meanwhile, in her new downtown location on 7th St., which she shares with dealers Harry Lunn, McIntosh/Drysdale, and Ramon Osuna, Brown continues to mount one-person shows by Washington sculptors Yuri Schwebler, Jim Sanborn, John Dickson, Nade Haley, Jenny Lea Knight, and Eric Rudd, along with artists of national and international reputation such as Loren Madsen, Lita Albuquerque, Brower Hatcher, Wade Saunders, Michael Todd, Peter Reginato, Alain Kirili of France, and Mark Brusse of Holland.

Brown also shows paintings by Robert Kitchen and realist Michel Hunter, along with paperworks by William Weegee, paintings by Ed Mayo, and photographs by Frank Di Perna, Leland Rice, and Gregory Conniff.

Capricorn Capricorn Galleries 4849 Rugby Ave., Bethesda, Md. 657-3477 Tuesday-Saturday: 11-5 Tuesday thru Friday eves: 7-9 Sunday: 1-5

Proprietor Phil Desind is a mathematician with a passion for art, realist art in particular. For 16 years he has offered one of the largest, most varied accumulations of twentieth-century-American realist paintings, prints, and sculpture anywhere in the area. Even when abstraction reigned, back in the trendy sixties and early seventies, Desind steadfastly continued to show prints by John Taylor Arms, Will Barnet, George Bellows, Walt Kuhn, Martin Lewis, and Adolf Dehn, who had his last exhibition at Capricorn. Robert Riggs, a famous illustrator before World War II, was rescued from abject poverty in his final years by shows at Capricorn.

Because the prices of those prints were so low (Desin never raised his prices even as the market rose), most have now been bought up by collectors and more price-savvy dealers who have since sold them, probably several times over. Desind, however, never at a loss to find new talent, has moved on, and over the past decade, with the resurgence of good new realist art, has finally hit his stride. Roger Medearis (protégé of Thomas Hart Benton), Vincent Arcilesi, Robert Birmelin, John Baeder (painter of diners), Harvey Dinnerstein, John Ingle, David Kessler, Daniel Lang, and Richard Pitts are just a few of the long list of artists of established or growing national reputation currently represented in the large stock.

Prints and drawings by Richard Haas, Michael Kirk, Cyril David, and George Staempfli are among the many fine graphic works. Trompe l'oeil art, always a sub-specialty here, is up-to-date in the carved wooden "objects"—everything from full-sized tables to ice skates and baseball mitts—by Roy Caravaglia and fool-the-eye paintings by Paul Sarkisian, Ernest Albert Land, Sam Cady, and Dahlia Ramanauskas.

Desind's gallery is still the same joyous jumble it has always been, despite a move to the ground floor of a new building in 1979, and passion for realism still sometimes surpasses a concern for top quality. But there are always enough pleasures—and occasional astonishments—to make the trek to Bethesda worthwhile for lovers of both traditional and contemporary realism.

Gallery-goers should note that the Bethesda Art Gallery, which specializes in early-twentieth-century American prints, is just around the corner.

Ewing Kathleen Ewing Gallery 3020 K St. NW 965-3133 Tuesday-Saturday: 11-6 Open by appointment only in August

For lovers of good, contemporary photography, Kathleen Ewing's gallery is well worth seeking out. It is located in a red brick building on the river side of K St., at the foot of 31st St. in Georgetown.

Devoted at first to representing and publishing an outstanding group of Washington photographers—Steve Szabo, Mark Power, Allen Appel, and Joe Cameron—Ewing now also shows talent from elsewhere, notably Christopher James from Boston, Arthur Ollman from San Francisco, and the extraordinary French still-life photographer Philippe Blache.

Along with a changing monthly program of shows by contemporaries, Ewing also exhibits some historic material, including work from the estate of Baltimore photographer A. Aubrey Bodine (1906-70) who concentrated on old sailing ships on the Chesapeake Bay and the life there. She also keeps some inexpensive vintage material on hand, ranging from images of old English cathedrals to nineteenth-century Venice. Other treasures, like Karl Struss's little-known nostalgic images of New York and San Francisco between 1909-29 can also be found. An experimental filmmaker, Struss, now 96, is the only surviving member of Stieglitz's Photo-Secession group.

Before opening her gallery, Ewing was a private dealer in Washington for several years.

Fendrick Fendrick Gallery 3059 M St. NW 338-4544 Monday-Saturday: 10-5 Closed August 15 to Labor Day

The Fendrick Gallery is known throughout the country as one of Washington's finest. Anyone who wants to see some of the best current American art in a broad range of media will find a visit to this three-story Georgetown establishment worthwhile.

Starting in the sixties, Barbara Fendrick brought the first shows of major artists like Rauschenberg, Johns, Dine, Frankenthaler, and

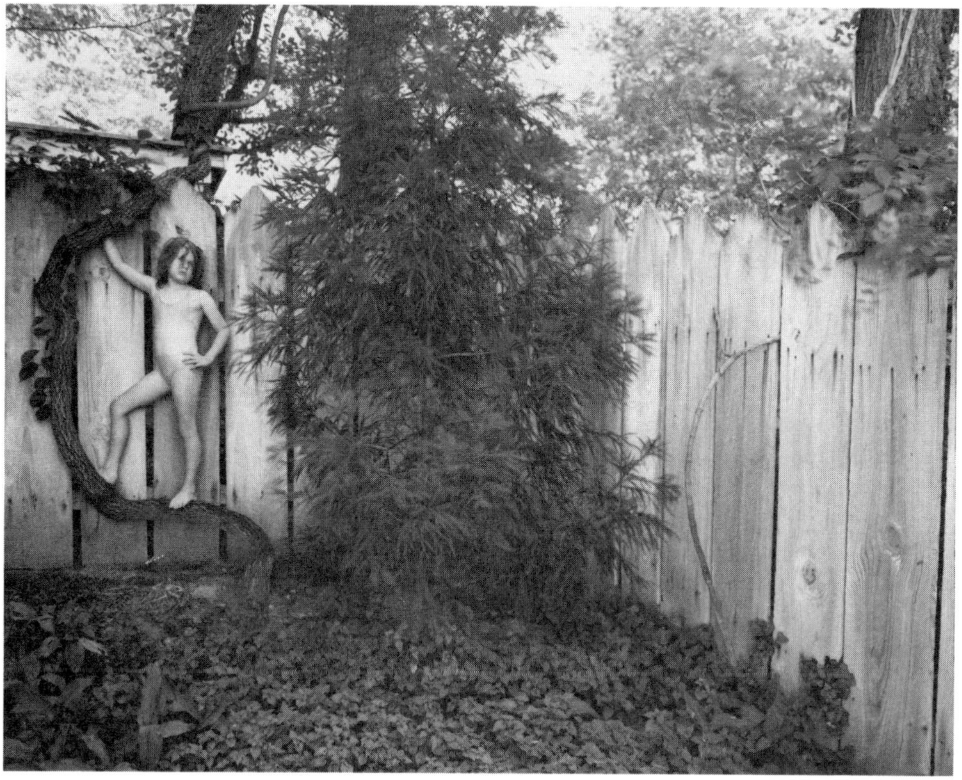

Shelagh by Mark Power. 8'' x 10'' palladium photograph. Kathleen Ewing.

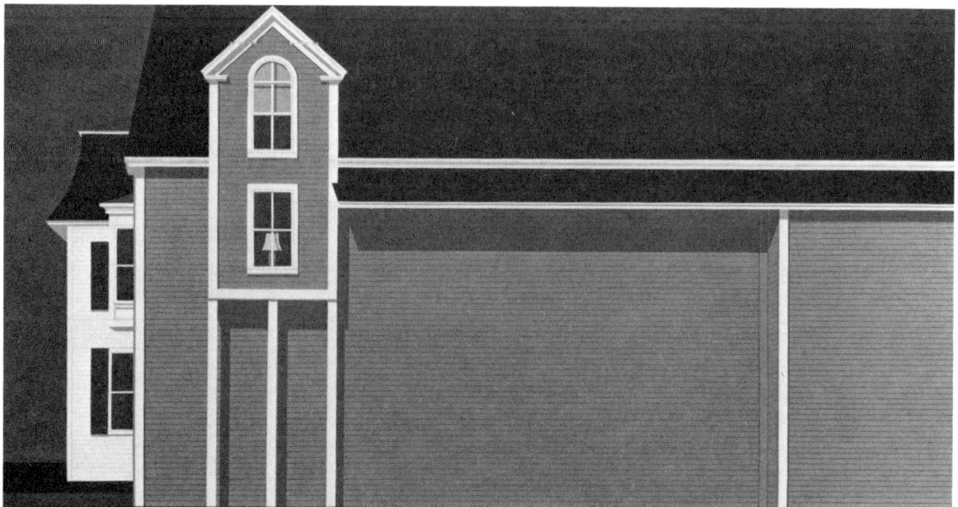

Yellow on Main Street by A Brockie Stevenson. 45'' x 84'' acrylic on canvas. Fendrick Gallery.

Motherwell to Washington, in the form of fine, small-edition graphics and works on paper. Since then she has constantly expanded her range to include paintings, drawings, watercolors, ceramics, glass, and decorative arts by top artists and craftsmen. The influential still-life painter, realist William Bailey, for example, is on the current roster. So is the kooky California ceramic sculptor and self-portraitist Robert Arneson.

There are also giant watercolor landscapes by Joseph Raffael and Patricia Forrester of California, and paintings by Daniel Brush, Brockie Stevenson, and James Pernotto that span the distance from abstraction to funk. Fendrick also has a whimsical streak, which brings us to the offbeat art of object-maker Barton Benes, funny ceramic ostriches by Bill Suworoff, and giant sculptural fantasy animals by Joan Danziger.

Master furniture-maker Wendell Castle, wrought-iron sculptor Albert Paley, fiber artist Sirpa Yarmolinsky, and glass-makers Dale Chihuly and Tom Patti represent some of the best talent currently at work in the decorative arts.

Exhibitions change monthly and are often ambitious group shows, such as "The Book as Art" and "Couples in Art."

Fiedler Barbara Fiedler Gallery 1621-21st St. NW 797-7131 Tuesday-Saturday: 11-5 Closed the last three weeks in August

This town-house gallery, not far from the Phillips Collection, can be easily spotted by the Yuri Schwebler sculpture that graces the tiny front lawn. After five years in business, Fiedler continues to show a varied group of contemporary artists, about half of them from Washington. Among the better-known sculptors represented by the gallery are Betty Parsons (the New York dealer), Dorothy Dehner, John Cunningham, V. V. Rankine, and H. I. Gates. Painters include Dorothy Preston, Wil Brunner, Elliott Thompson, Carroll Sockwell, Stephen Pace, Pat Adams, and papermaker Andrea Way.

In addition to changing shows on the main floor, Fiedler keeps a large assortment of smaller works upstairs, among them the drawings of Constance Costigan and political cartoonist Vint Lawrence, and the small boxes of Madolin Cervantes.

Capitol East Capitol East Graphics 600 E St. SE 547-8246 Saturday and Sunday: 2-6 and by appointment

After a year in business on Capitol Hill, this gallery strives to bring to the attention of a wider public the prints and sculpture of contemporary Afro-American and European artists. Many of the exhibitions, though not all, focus on Afro-American artists who have not been widely shown, among them printmakers Earl Miller from Seattle, Sharon Sutton and Vincent Smith from New York; Norma Morgan from Woodstock, N.Y.; Alonzo Davis from Los Angeles; and Madeline Rabb from Chicago. Well-known artists Romare Bearden, Jacob Lawrence, James Wells, and Herbert Gentry are also included in the portfolios of H. Elaine Jackson, the gallery's owner and founder.

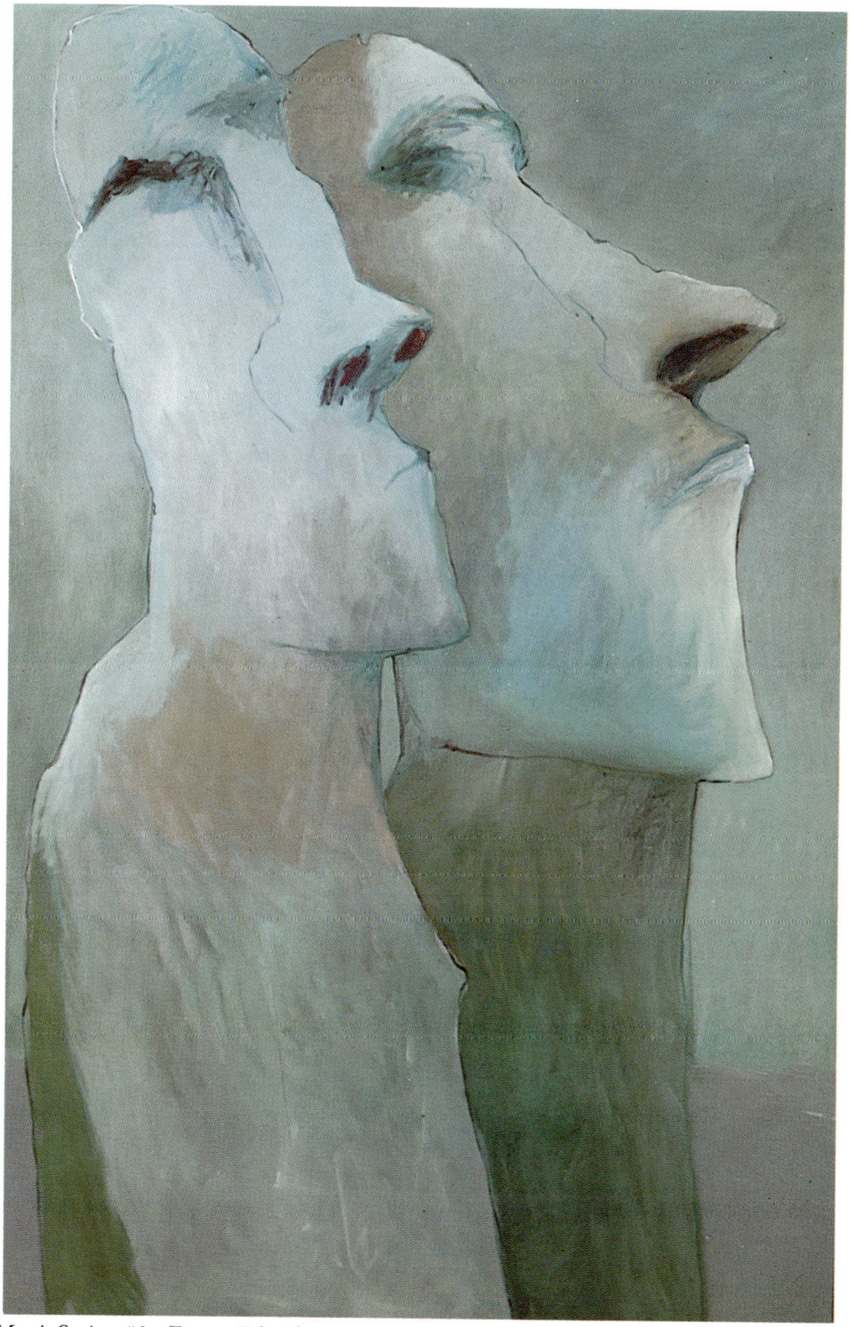

Moai Series #3, Easter Island, 1980, by Dorothy Preston. 72½'' x 48'' oil on canvas. Barbara Fiedler Gallery.

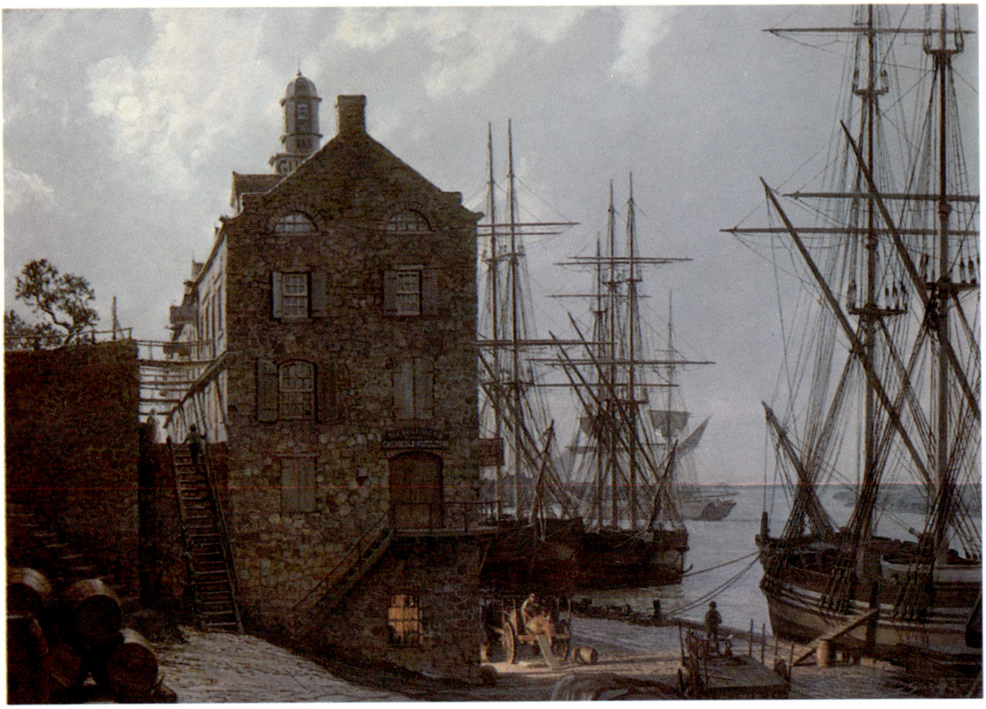

Savannah, River Street in 1842 by Moonlight by John Stobart. 20'' x 28½'' lithograph. Atlantic Gallery.

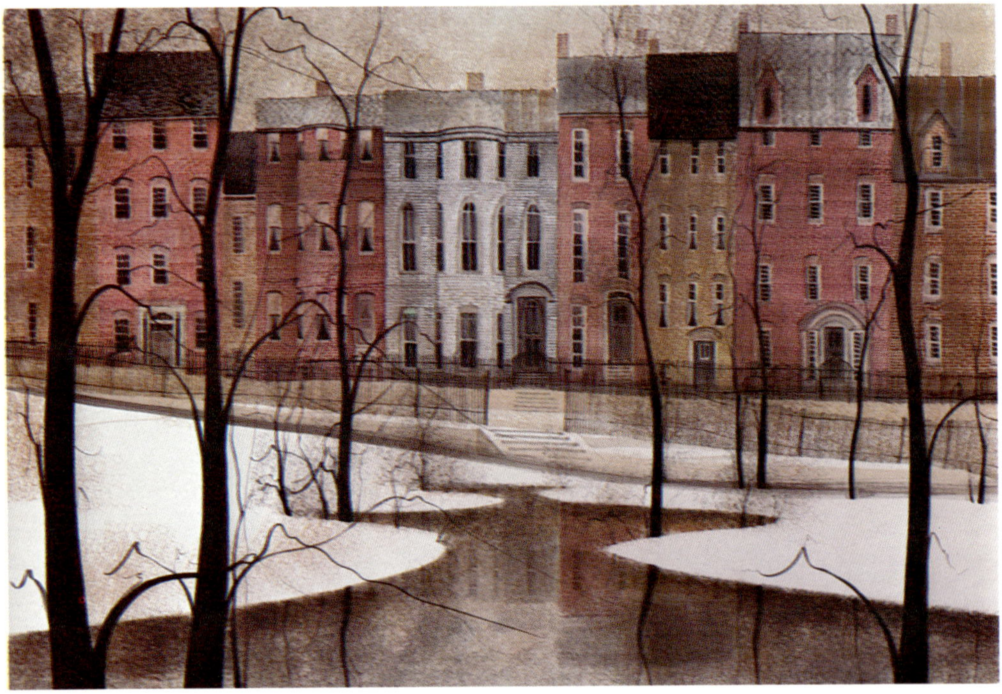

The Street by the Park by P. Buckley Moss. 30'' x 40'' watercolor. The Moss Portfolio, Atlantic Gallery.

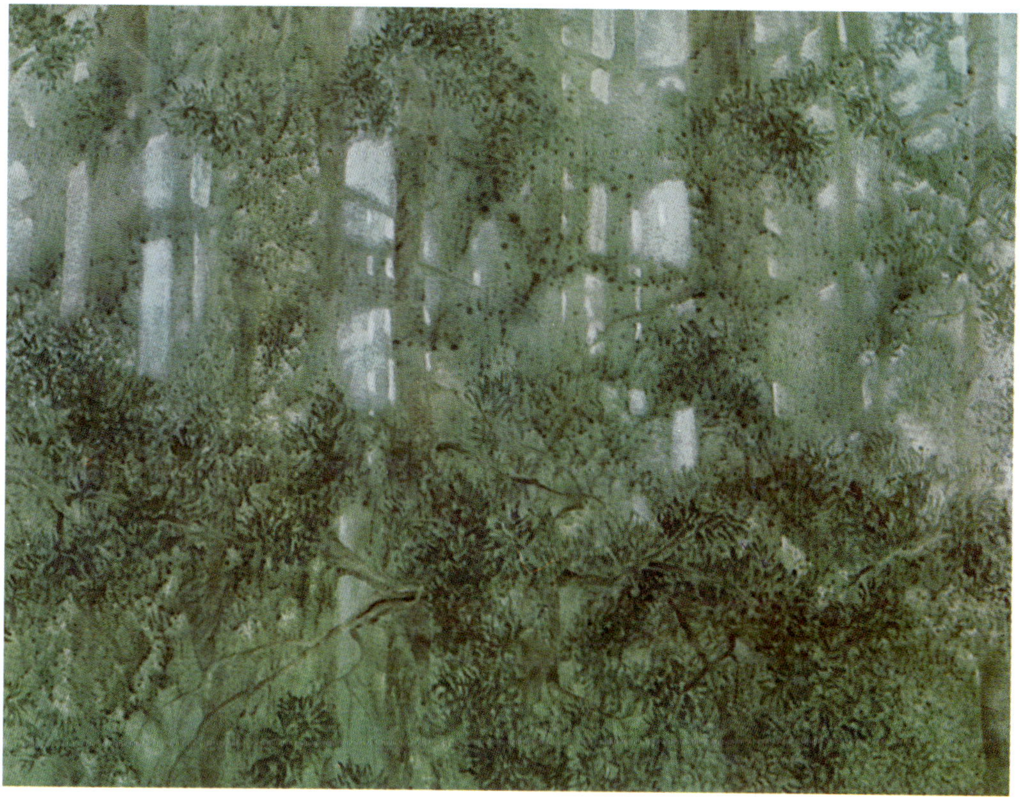

Light in the Forest by Lee Weiss. Watercolor. Franz Bader Gallery.

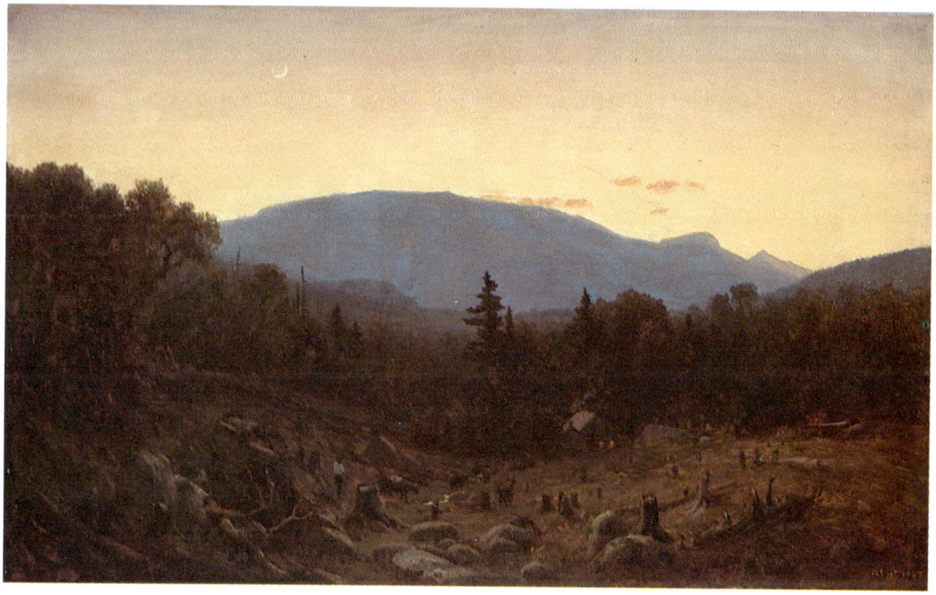

Twilight on Hunter Mountain, 1865, by Sanford Gifford. 10¼'' x 17'' oil on canvas. Adams Davidson Gallery.

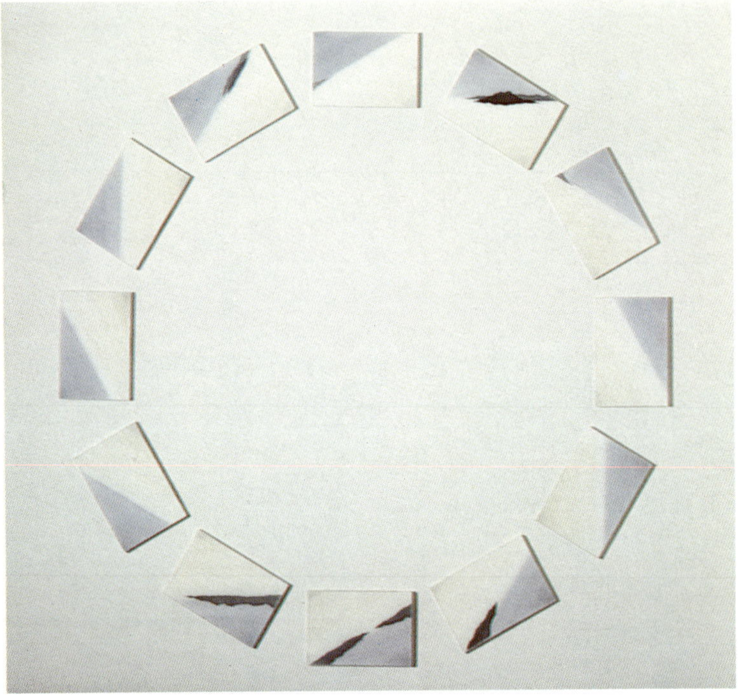

O #3 by Ed Mayo. 7½'' x 11'' (each frame), 66'' diameter, acrylic/plexiglass. Diane Brown Gallery.

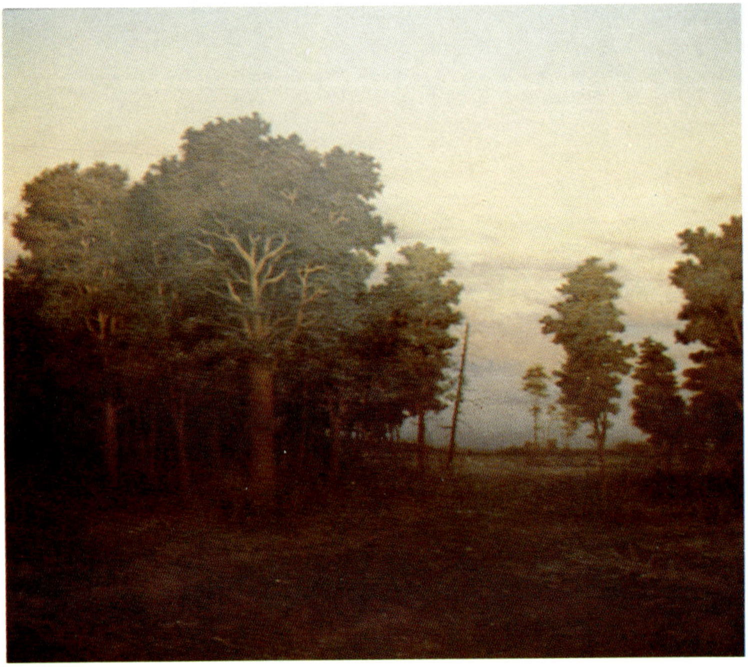

September by Anthony Watkins. 29'' x 34'' oil on canvas. Tolley Fine Arts.

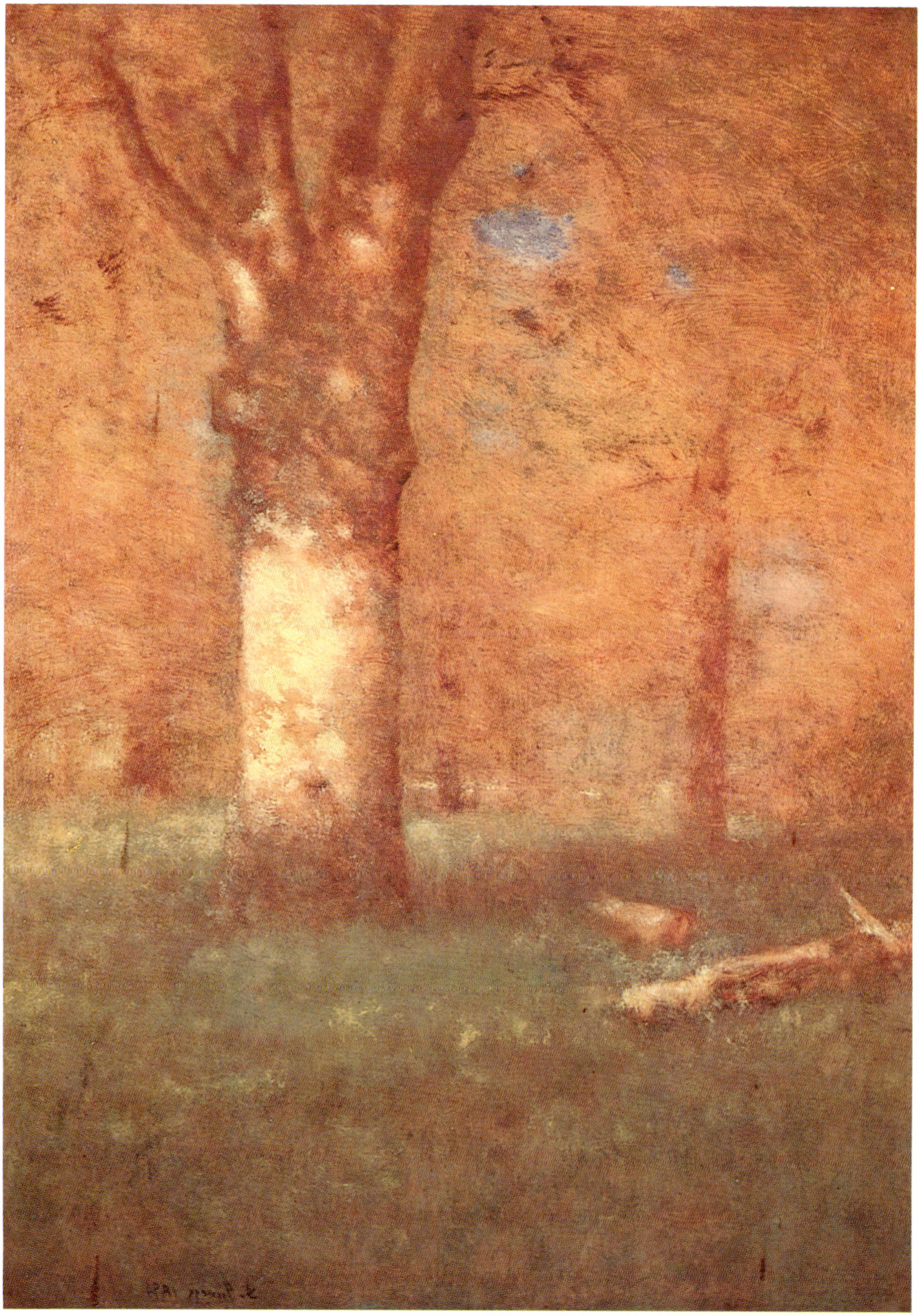

The Beeches, 1894, by George Inness. 42'' x 32'' oil on canvas. Adams Davidson Gallery.

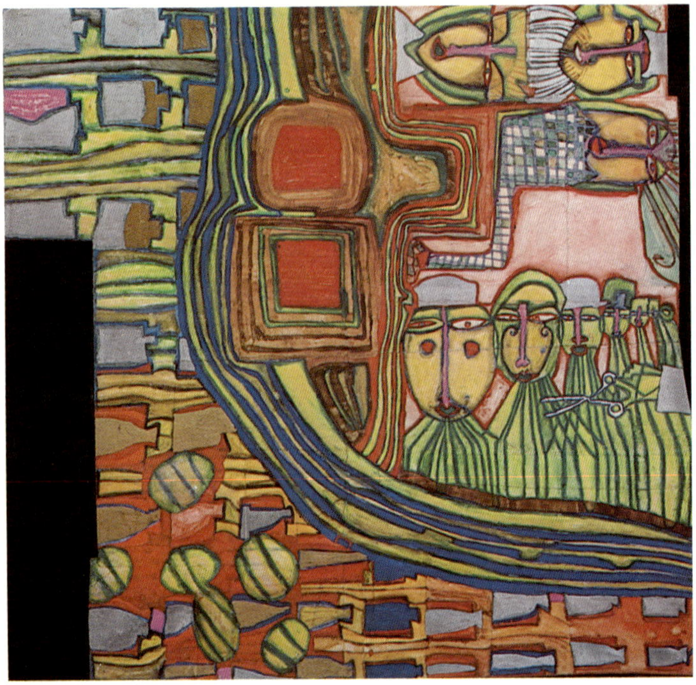

Hairdresser's Heaven by Friedensreich Hundertwasser. 16½'' x 14¾'' watercolor & mixed media. Baumgartner Gallery.

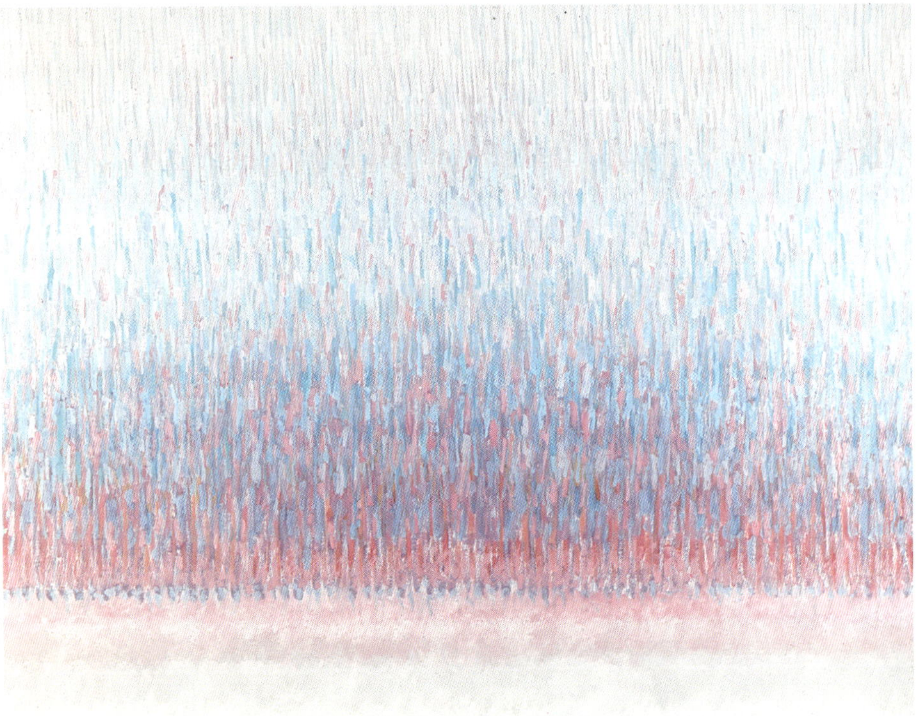

Horizon by Hilda Thorpe. 84'' x 108'' acrylic on canvas. Gallery 4.

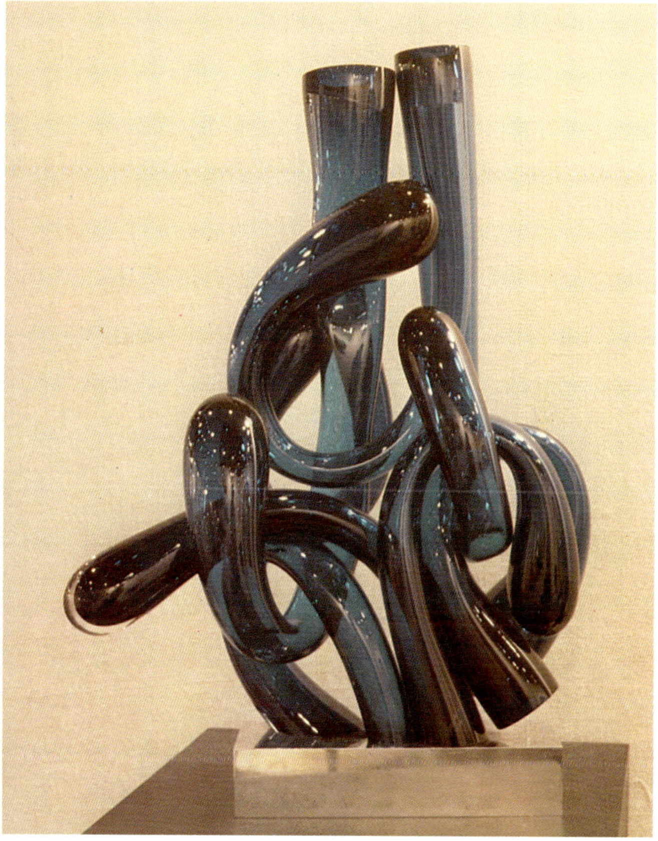

Untitled Sculpture by Kent F. Ipsen. 25¾'' x 18½'' x 6'' blown glass. Glass Gallery of Eveleth & Summerford, Associates.

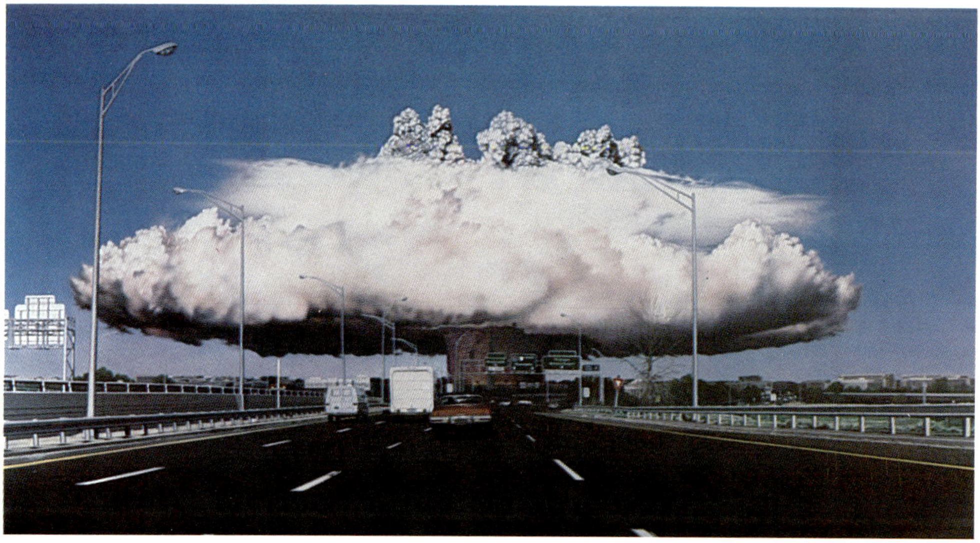

The Last Washington Painting by Alan Sonneman. 54'' x 102'' oil on canvas. Gallery K.

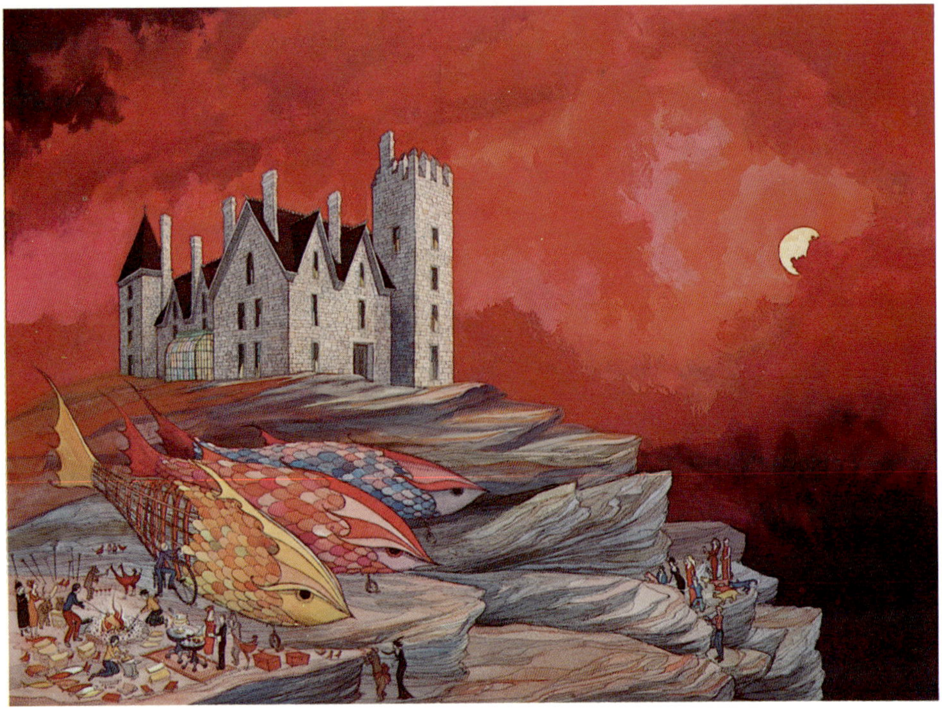

Fisherman's Holiday by Kenneth Koskela. 22'' x 30'' watercolor. Hallway Gallery.

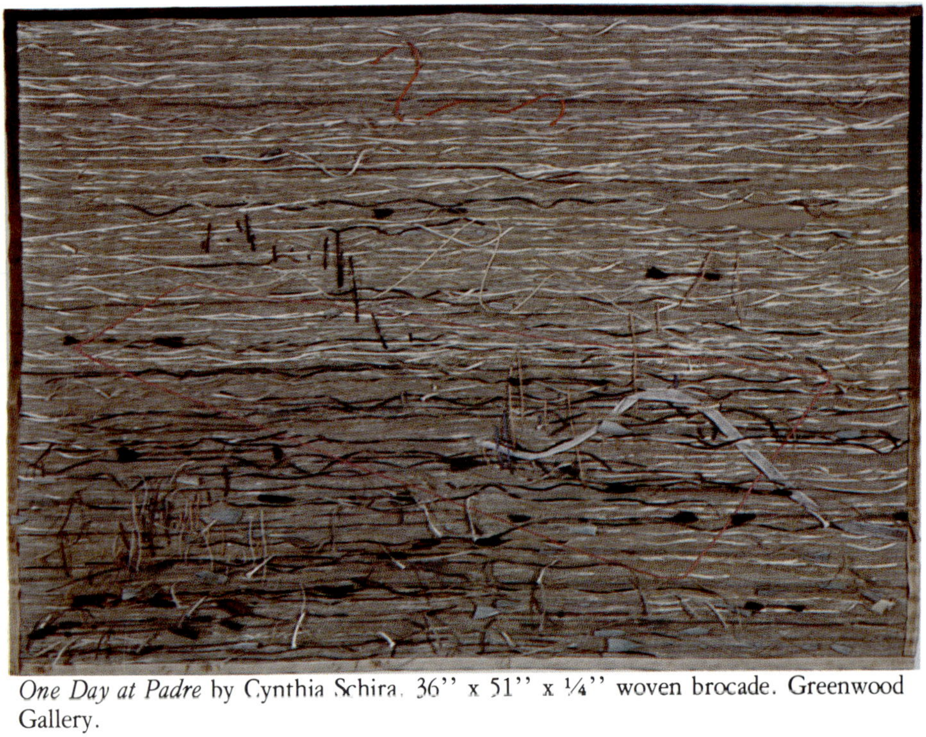

One Day at Padre by Cynthia Schira. 36'' x 51'' x ¼'' woven brocade. Greenwood Gallery.

Several printmakers from abroad are also featured, including Bengt Lindstrom from Sweden, Mexican-American Elizabeth Catlett, Algerian Michel Mathonnat, and Yugoslav artists Joze Ciuha, Adriana Maraz, and Janez Bernik. Washington printmaker Jack Perlmutter is also represented here.

Fondo del Sol Fondo del Sol Visual Art & Media Center 2112 R St. NW 483-2777 Wednesday-Saturday: 12:30-6:30

This nonprofit gallery and community arts center is part of a growing national network of alternative spaces devoted to spotlighting the new energies being injected into current American art by Hispanic artists—Latino, Chicano, and Puerto Rican—as well as by native Americans, Afro-Americans, and other minorities. This former three-story house, near the Phillips Collection, houses not only exhibition galleries but workshop spaces for painting and video. It is one of the few places in Washington where new work in video can always be viewed.

The Center opened in 1977 with grants from the Cafritz Foundation and the National Endowment for the Arts which continues its support. The D.C. Commission on the Arts & Humanities also supports the Center.

The exhibitions, which change monthly, are usually group shows, and some have subsequently toured. The inaugural "Roots & Visions," organized with the help of the National Collection of Fine Arts, was the first traveling show of contemporary work by Hispanic-American artists from all over the country, and it toured 20 museums. Luis Jiminez, Rafael Ferrer, Rafael Ortiz, Dino Aranda, and Larry Fuente are but a few of the 48 artists introduced in that revealing survey. Subsequent shows have featured work by Chilean exile artists now scattered all over the world, including Matta. There have been retrospectives of performance artist Jonas dos Santos and video artist Juan Downey; shows of French-speaking artists of Quebec and the Cajuns of Louisiana are in the works.

Video art plays a major role at Fondo del Sol, which, through Osiris Productions, produces as well as exhibits videotapes and films dealing with cultural and artistic heritage of the many cultures that comprise the Americas. Free video programs are offered every Saturday afternoon.

Gage Gage Gallery 3019 M St. NW 338-0034 Tuesday-Saturday: 11-8 Sunday: 1-5

This Georgetown print gallery, now two years old, is one of the few in town that deals exclusively with fine contemporary prints from all over the world, including Europe, the Orient, and North and South America. All are signed, numbered, small editions, in most cases pulled by the artists themselves. These are printmakers primarily, and are not to be confused with painters who do large, so-called limited editions on the side.

There are well-known names and accomplished lesser-knowns, among them the influential Johnny Friedlaender, Elie Abrahami and Tuvia

Beeri from Israel, Rene Carcan from Belgium, Mario Micossi from Italy, Luis Piza from Brazil and Hiroshi Asada from Japan. From France come two virtuoso printmakers, etcher Erik Desmazieres and copperplate engraver Philippe Mohlitz, along with Avati, Andre Bongibault, and Brigitte Coudrain. The Americans are Robert Kipniss, Robert Ecker, and Francisco Larez.

The couple who run the gallery tend to emphasize technical excellence in a broad range of styles. Their aim is to show good work at reasonable prices, which they do.

Foundry

Foundry Gallery 2121 P St. NW 296-0545 Tuesday-Saturday: 11-5 Closed August

Foundry began five years ago as a co-op, but has since become an artist-owned gallery devoted to showing work by a varied group of Washington artists. The owners—Lou Jones, Roxie Munro, Virginia Janotta, Margaret McBride, Shirley Koller, and Alan Weatherley—exhibit occasionally, but by no means exclusively, in the two-person monthly shows. The range in style and media is broad, from the amusing "Claudia Dolls" by conceptualist Claudia De Monte to landscapes and painterly realism by Henry Niece, both of whom teach at the University of Maryland.

Showing on a fairly regular basis are sculptors Tad Wanveer, Agnes Brodie, and Marie Ringwald, who does environmental work. Painters include emerging artists Judy Bass, Dale Appleman, Richard Klank, Susan Middleman, and Sandy Walker. Margot Kernan and Larry Bazel head the list of photographers.

The gallery also sometimes organizes major group shows.

Gallery 4

Gallery 4 115 S. Columbus St., Alexandria, Va. 548-4600 Tuesday-Saturday: 10-5 Closed August

One of Alexandria's best, Gallery 4 is devoted to showing good contemporary artists from the Washington area and elsewhere, among them Alexandria's own Hilda Thorpe, a sculptor of national stature currently working in handmade paper. Paintings by Charlotte Robinson, sculpture by Hildegarde van Roijen, watercolors and prints by Deborah Ellis, and collages by Lea Feinstein are also featured in changing monthly shows.

Among the many good prints featured here are silkscreens by photorealist Joseph Craig English, woodcuts by Gordon Mortensen, and etchings by Michael Jacques and Bruce McCombs, who specializes in nostalgic scenes of old automobiles. The gallery is owned by four area women.

Gallery 10

Gallery 10 1519 Connecticut Ave. NW 232-3326 Tuesday-Saturday: 11-5 Closed last three weeks in August

Founded in 1973, this gallery is a corporation owned by nine artists, but uses almost all of its exhibition time and space to show the work of others, most of them highly accomplished East Coast professionals who

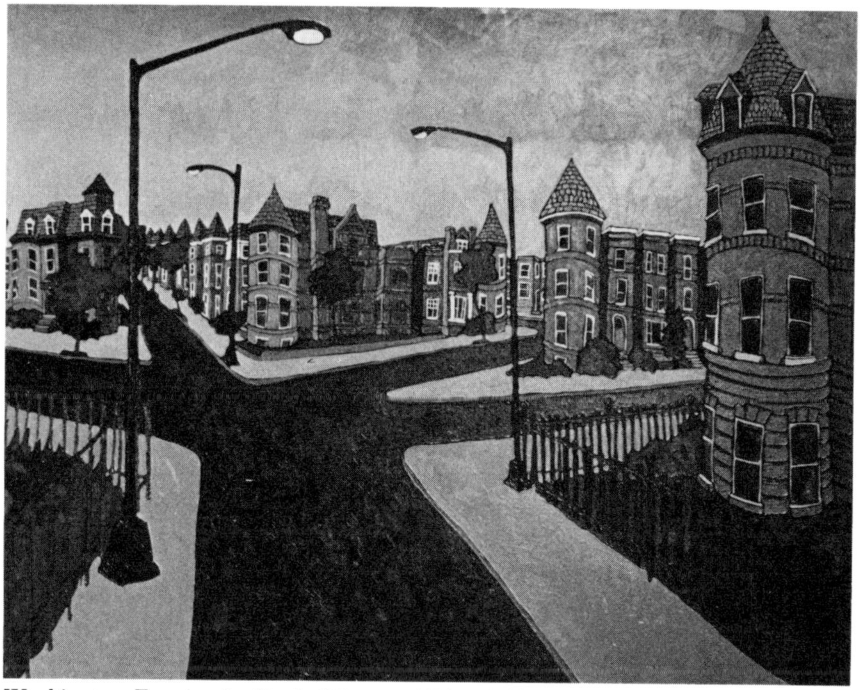

Washington Evening by Roxie Munro. 45'' x 60'' oil. Foundry Gallery.

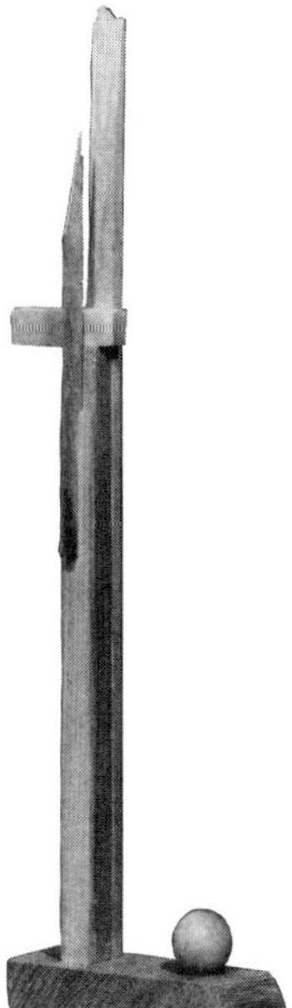

Guardian #1 1980 by Dorothy Dehner. 20'' x 1½'' x 5½'' various woods. Barbara Fiedler.

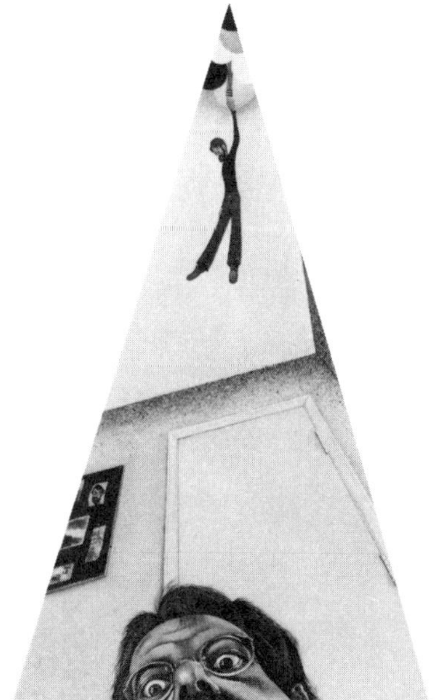

Triangle by Alan Weatherley. 19 1/4'' x 11 7/8'' watercolor on paper. Foundry Gallery.

deserve more attention than they've had to date. There is no particular "line," though shows tend to represent artists working in more advanced and experimental modes.

Originality of vision in a wide range of traditional and nontraditional media is particularly admired here, and, as a result the gallery has catapulted several new talents into the national arena, notably sculptors Nade Haley, David Staton, Tom Rooney, Dickson Carroll, Carla Rosenzweig, and the mysterious Susan Harvey from Georgia. Rebecca Kamen, Robert Fergerson, Noche Crist, environmental sculptor Marie Ringwald, Marianne LaRoche, and the provocative new printmaker Richard Powell have also had first solos here.

Each year Gallery 10 organizes an ambitious theme show, in addition to solos and duos, based on one medium—e.g., wood, paper or "boxes," —bringing together many area artists, known and unknown. Catalogues are always published. The gallery has a healthy sales record, and asks no exclusive arrangements from artists it chooses to exhibit.

Gallery H

Gallery H 4923 Bethesda Ave., Bethesda, Md. 656-9444 Monday-Friday: 10-6 Saturday: 11-5

The unassuming facade of this year-old gallery belies its pleasant, ample, and well-lit interior space. Located one flight up, not far from downtown Bethesda, the gallery focuses on works by lesser-known area artists, with an emphasis on contemporary Asian-Americans. The owner is Korean artist Hangok Chang, who makes handsome shoji screens when she is not making her ink paintings on cloth and rice paper.

Gallery K

Gallery K 2032 P St. NW 223-6955 Tuesday-Friday: 11-6

Established in 1976 by Washington collector and dealer Marc Moyens and Komei Wachi, this gallery has a special interest in figurative art with surrealist overtones, and shows contemporary artists, known and unknown, from all over the U.S. and abroad. Seven languages are spoken here.

Among the good East Coast painters exhibited in monthly shows are James Baumgardner, Robert McCurdy, Bernard Martin, Jody Mussoff, Alan Sonneman, Barbara Frank, Fred Folsom, Bill Newman, and Robert Hynes. The owners' vast collection of over 4,000 works is also part of the stock, and includes works by Lindner, Matta, Motherwell, Rauschenberg, Warhol, Thiebaud, Nicholson, and more. These works can be seen, by appointment only, at an annex the gallery maintains at 2129 Florida Ave., NW.

Georgetown

Georgetown Art Gallery 2611 P St. NW 333-5824 Tuesday-Saturday: 11-5:30 Closed mid-July through August

This tiny establishment is located between the P Street Strip and Georgetown and organizes increasingly good monthly shows. With a clear bias toward traditional figurative still-life and landscape painters, it has introduced several from the area over the past four years. Gerald Wartof-

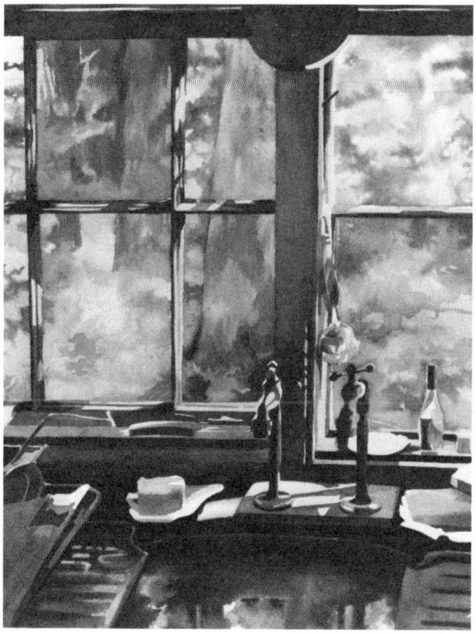

Sink in Maine by Deborah Ellis. 21'' x 16½'' watercolor. Gallery 4.

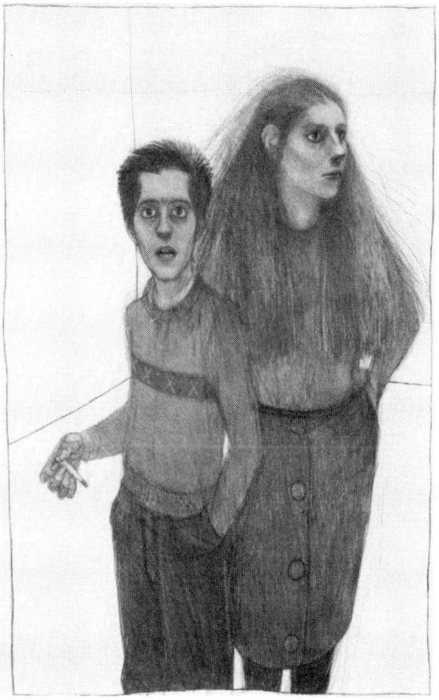

Pamela & Joie by Jody Mussoff. 40'' x 28'' color pencil. Gallery K.

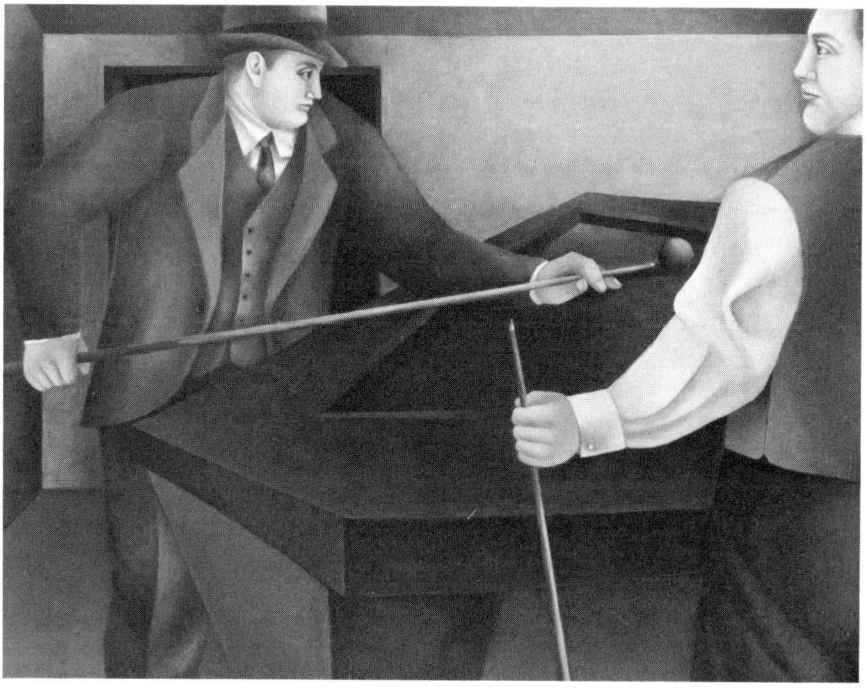

Pool Players by Richard Lindner. 35'' x 46'' oil on canvas. Gallery K.

sky, Carleton Fletcher, Sandra Walker, Larry Chappelear, John Morrell, Michael Francis, and Sherry Kasten are among the best, with collagist Lea Feinstein leading the short list of nonfigurative artists.

Glass Glass Gallery of Eveleth & Summerford 4918 Del Ray Ave., Bethesda, Md. 652-4999 Tuesday-Friday: 11-4 Saturday: 11-5

This small room at the rear of a fine suburban antiques shop has been showing new work in studio glass since the renaissance in that medium began a decade ago. Other galleries have since chimed in, but antiques/glass dealer Sarah Eveleth continues to show many of the best. Henry Halem, Audrey Handler, Kent Ipsen, Jon Kuhn, Tom McGlauchlin, and Sylvia Vigiletti are all on view, and were included in the recent survey, "New Glass," organized by the Corning Museum and shown in 1980 at the Renwick Gallery in Washington.

The gallery also shows up-and-coming talents like Corey Powers, Jon and Deb Meyer, Kathleen Mulcahy, and Mark Russell. The focus is on nonfunctional container forms, sculpture, and commissioned pieces.

Govinda Govinda Gallery 1227-34th St. NW 333-1180 Tuesday-Saturday: 11-5 Closed August

Proprietors Kim and Chris Murray, both young artist-illustrators, have devoted the past five years to showing an unusual mix of new talent that ranges from contemporary Russian icons to contemporary British illustrators. This small Georgetown gallery, located away from most of the others, limits itself to paintings, drawings, and prints, with a special interest in visionary art and current book illustration.

There have been some offbeat shows, one featuring contemporary work by a Ukrainian-born restorer of old Russian icons at Dumbarton Oaks, Roman Bukowinsky, and another of atmospheric landscapes by Alexis de Boeck, a horticulturist at Dumbarton Oaks. Michael Knigin, an amusing New York printmaker who crosses famous Japanese woodblocks with Pop Art, had his first solo here, as have Washington landscape painters Howard Carr and Martin Kotler.

Graphic Antiquity Graphic Antiquity 1214-31st St. NW 965-8988 Tuesday-Saturday: 10:30-6

Located just opposite the Georgetown Post Office, this tiny gallery deals in original but inexpensive late 19th century vintage photographs of people and places, famous and infamous, from America and abroad. What distinguishes this material from the higher-priced vintage photography market is that here the subject matter is primary, rather than the name of the photographer or assured rarity. For history buffs, the shop is a must.

The owners are Cliff and Michele Krainik, who for 10 years ran a successful vintage photography catalogue business in Chicago before opening their Washington shop in summer of 1980. There are bins and drawers filled with nicely matted and carefully researched daguerrotypes,

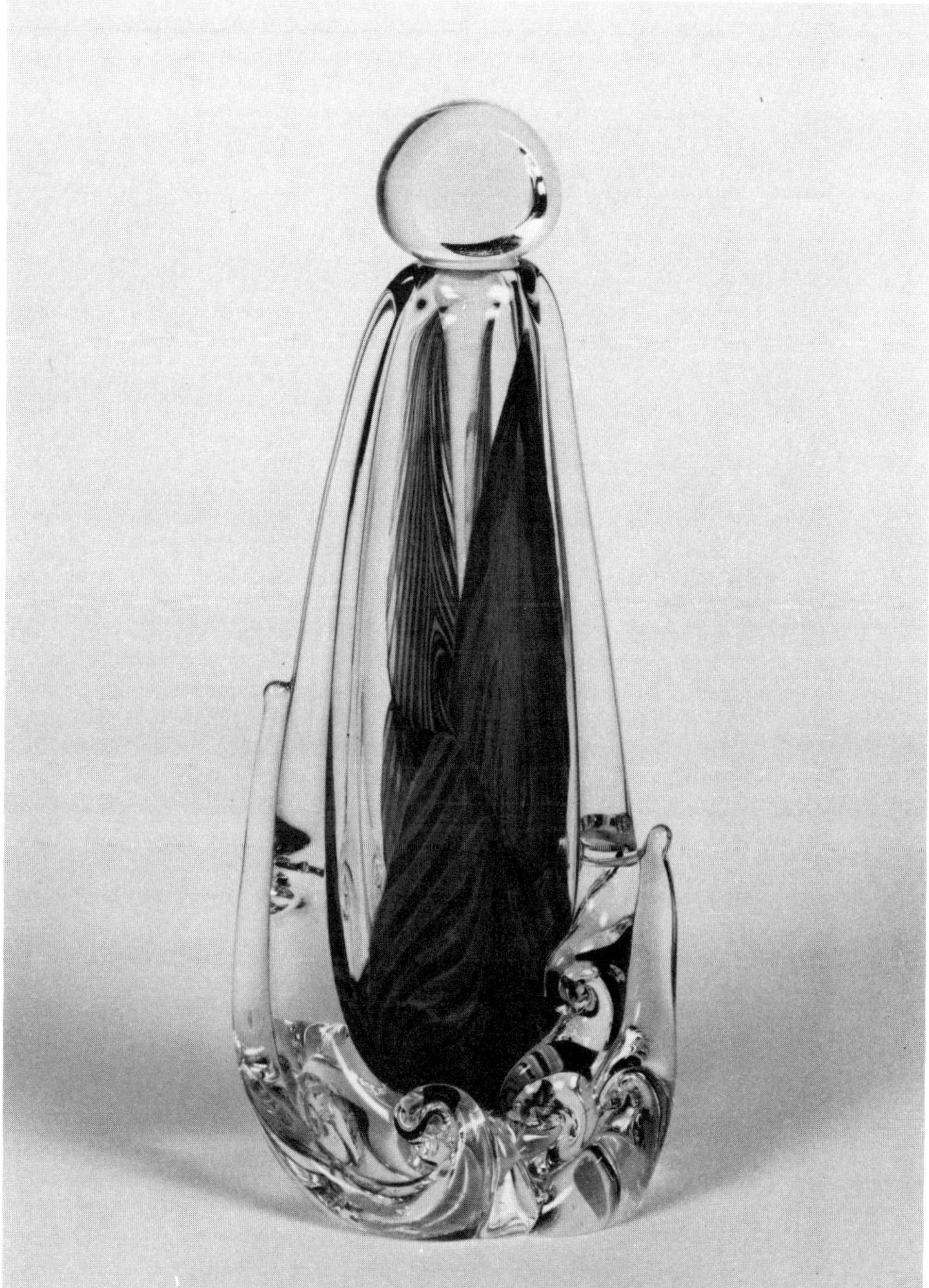

Stoppered Sentinel Form by Audrey Handler. 7'' blown glass. Glass Gallery, Eveleth & Summerfod Associates.

tintypes, stereographs, large albumen prints and hundreds of "Cartes de Visite"—images printed between 1860 and 1890, when they were all the rage world-wide. Mathew Brady, the great Civil War photographer, set up a shop on Pennsylvania Ave. where he made "cartes" for everyone from Abraham Lincoln to John Wilkes Booth and his brother, the actor Edwin Booth. Their images can usually be found in stock.

Photographs of Lillie Langtry have also been seen here, along with those of Oliver Wendell Holmes, Louis Pasteur, the original Tom Thumb, and the famed Siamese twins Chang and Eng Bunker. Early photographs of black cowboys, Indians and the American west; the Middle East and Asia; early balloon flight and the city of Washington in the 1890's are all likely to be found here at reasonable prices.

Greenwood Greenwood Gallery 2014 P St. NW 833-2910 Monday-Saturday: 10-6

As evidence of the recent surge of both interest and high creativity in the crafts field, several new galleries have opened in Washington, dealing primarily with the work of artist-craftsmen. Greenwood appears to be one of the best.

"We're here to educate both the artisan and the lay public and make clear that the state of the art has gone far beyond the mugs in the pot shop," says Carolyn Hecker, gallery director and former program co-ordinator at the Smithsonian. "There are other things besides paintings, prints, and photographs that are art and collectible."

To prove their point, Greenwood opened in spring of 1980 with works by 70 leading American contemporary craft artists, including master furniture-makers Wendell Castle and Robert Whitley, ceramic artists Peter Voulkos and Paul Soldner; tapestry-maker Cynthia Schira; and basket-maker John McQueen. Others scheduled for future shows are glass artists Marvin Lipofsky and Fritz Dreisbach, and fiber artist Barbara Shawcroft.

Gerhardt Knodel, head of the fiber department at Cranbrook Academy, ceramic artist Richard Shaw, and metal artists Stanley Lechtzin and Albert Paley are among the many leading artist craftsmen scheduled to give workshops for artists in area universities under the sponsorship of the gallery.

EMC, Inc. (Environmental Management Consultants) is a group of architects and engineers supporting both the gallery and workshop programs.

Hallway Hallway Gallery 3235 P St. NW 965-0442 Tuesday-Saturday: 10-5

This very small Georgetown gallery shows a variety of contemporary paintings, drawings, and prints from all over the country, many with the look of fairy-tale illustration. There are fantasy paintings by Kenneth Koskela, fantasy lithographs by David Driesbach, surreal watercolors by Mary Hartmann, and genre scenes by Tom McKinney. There are also mezzotints by G. H. Rothe showing ballet dancers, surreal landscapes,

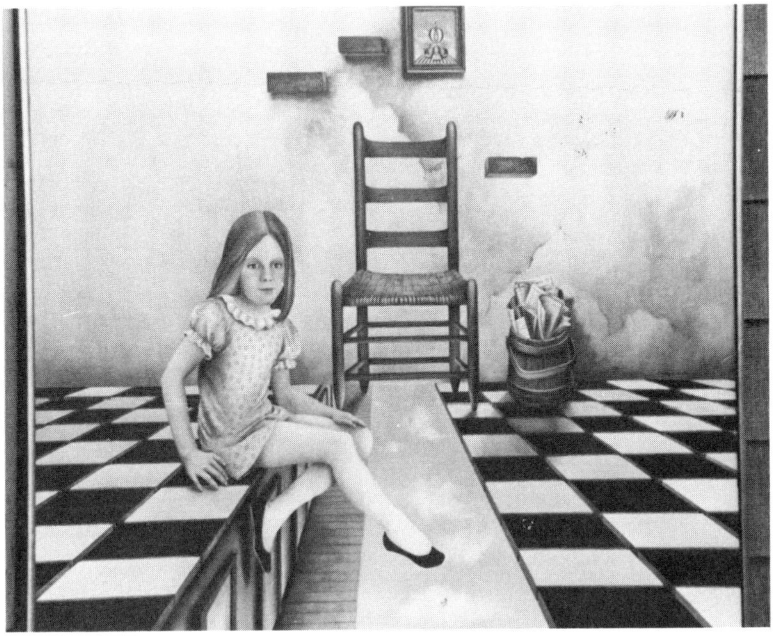

Monday's Tuesday by Terry Alaimo. 36'' x 32'' oil on canvas. Hallway Gallery.

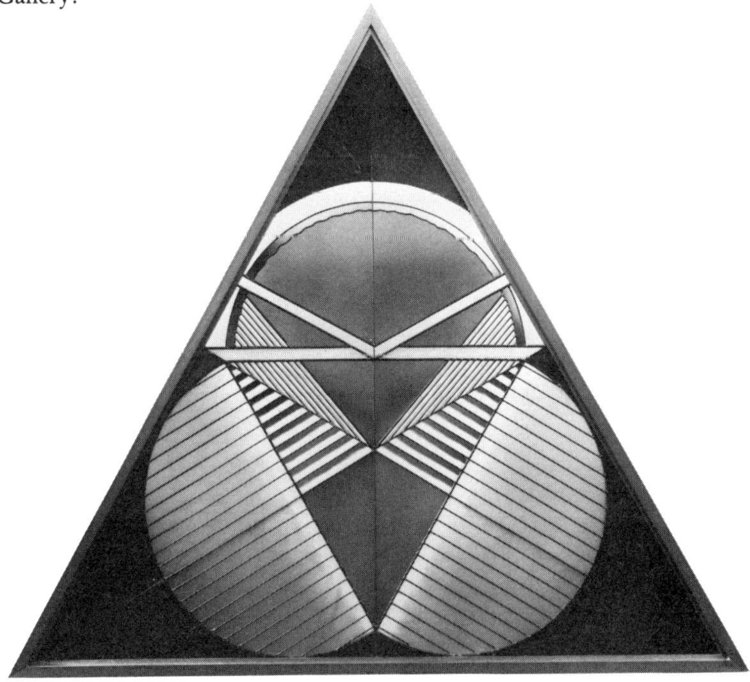

Reflective Triangle by Ray King. 83'' x 96'' x 19'' (with base) freestanding stained glass and metal sculpture. Greenwood Gallery.

and florals. Edward Sokol's serigraphs, George Carpenter's Maine landscapes and seascapes, Joel Beckwith's biting, satirical etchings, and Thea Tewi's abstract marble sculptures are also always on view.

Haslem Jane Haslem Gallery 2121 P St. NW 338-3014 Tuesday-Saturday: 10-5

One of Washington's longest-running contemporary art establishments—and still one of the best after two decades—Haslem specializes in American art from 1900 to the present, with emphasis on fine prints by the best-known innovators since World War II: Mauricio Lasansky, Gabor Peterdi, Antonio Frasconi, Leonard Baskin, Misch Kohn, Michael Ponce de Leon, and Rudy Pozzatti. Will Barnet and Mark Tobey are also represented by Haslem.

The gallery has a wide selection of the next generation of printmakers as well, notably Richard Ziemann and Michael Mazur, along with Steven Barbash, Anthony Gorny, and David Itchkawich. Two realist painters show here: the widely known Billy Morrow Jackson and Washingtonian John Winslow.

Haslem is among the handful of galleries in the country that deal in original political cartoons and comic strips by Tony Auth, Pat Oliphant, Jules Feiffer, and Gary Trudeau, to mention only a few among dozens listed in the catalog of available work.

This large, handsome space features monthly shows, and often circulates exhibitions to museums and galleries elsewhere. It is located just off the lobby of the Georgetown House Hotel, in the middle of P St. Strip.

Henri Henri Gallery 1500-21st St. NW 659-9313 Tuesday-Saturday: 11-6 Sunday: 2-6

The longest-running gallery on the P St. Strip is operated by Henrietta Ehrsam, who moved to Washington from Alexandria in 1967, after running a successful avant-garde gallery there for a decade.

Henri, as this popular dealer is called, has always preferred the way-out, which a decade ago included Washington color painters like Gene Davis and Tom Downing and sculptor Ed McGowin. Since then she has continued to turn up new and unusual work by artists from all over, some of the best being sculptors Robert Stackhouse, John Van Alstine, Stanislav Kolibal of Czechoslovakia, Bob Jensen (who makes huge ceramic objects, including surfboards), Michael Bigger, Peter Charles, Robert Bourdon, and Lester Van Winkle (who makes improbable furniture).

Henri also shows paintings, all abstract, by Tom Holcomb, Traute Ishida, Tom Nakashima, Jim Sullivan and Leslie Exton. Color photographer Graeme Outerbridge from Bermuda has also shown here.

This is one of the most welcoming galleries in town, and always worth a visit for nontraditionalists.

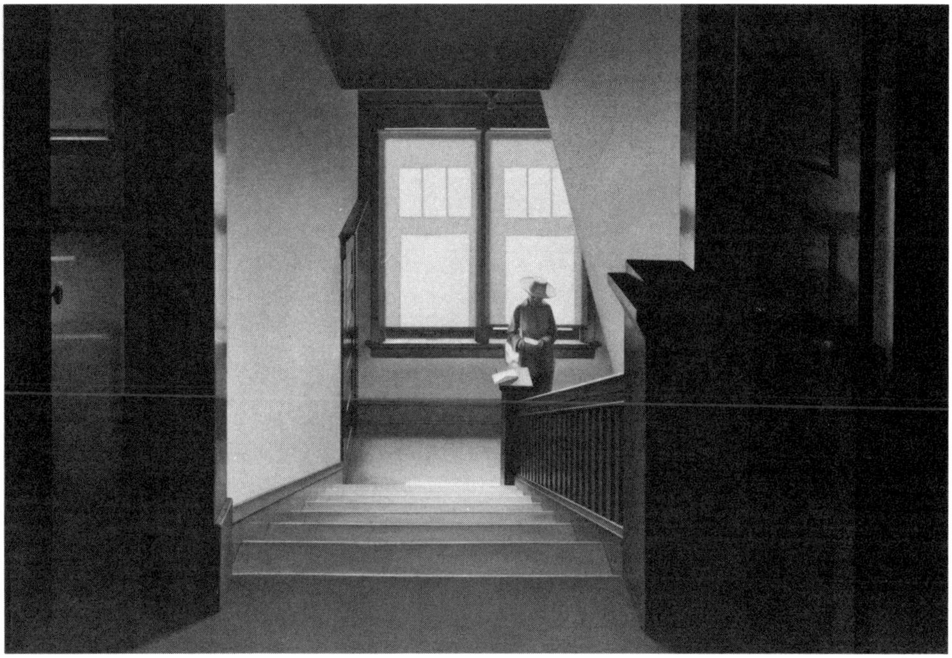

Ten O Nine 1975 by Billy Morrow Jackson. 48'' x 72'' oil on masonite. Jane Haslem Gallery.

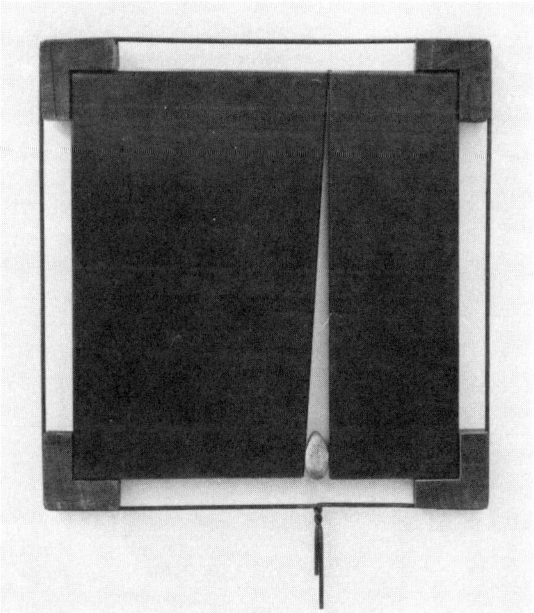

Untitled by Peter Charles. Black walnut, rock and steel. Henri Gallery.

Hom Gallery 2103 O St. NW 466-4976 Tuesday-Saturday: 11-5

This world-class print gallery specializes in turn-of-the-century European masters like Matisse, Gauguin, Cézanne, Toulouse-Lautrec, Paul Klee and Edvard Munch, as well as early-twentieth-century American masters like John Sloan, Martin Lewis, Max Weber, Maurice Prendergast, James McNeill Whistler, Childe Hassam, Edward Hopper, Elie Nadelman, and Louis Lozowick. Hom sometimes also has drawings, paintings, and sculpture by these artists.

The gallery represents only one contemporary artist, Washington wood and marble sculptor Leonard Cave, though others may be added in this new space, which quadruples Hom's former P St. quarters. Though the gallery will continue to focus on the graphic arts, Hom also plans to expand into more works on paper and paintings.

A highly respected dealer in the area for sixteen years, Hom publishes an annual catalog of his inventory. He often represents the interests of museums, other dealers, and collectors at print auctions all over the world.

Hull Hull Gallery 3301 New Mexico Ave. NW 362-0507 Monday-Saturday: 1-5 Wednesday: till 7 Closed last three weeks in August

Located in Foxhall Square, an indoor office-shopping complex, this pleasant two-room gallery has managed to mix good exhibitions of nineteenth- and early-twentieth-century works on paper with shows by American contemporaries, most of whom paint or print or draw in a lyrical, traditional, or semi-abstract vein. Nature-lover Alan Gussow has shown his paintings here, as has Susan Davis, the popular Washington illustrator who also makes sunny pastel drawings. Sandy Walker, Reeve Schley, Susan Harvey, Mary Betts Anderson, Brenda Star, and John Himmelfarb are other contemporaries represented by Hull.

The early twentieth-century American works—mostly drawings, watercolors, and prints—are a big draw, and Childe Hassam, Everett Shinn, William Glackens, George Bellows, Charles Burchfield, Oscar Bluemner, Reginald Marsh, Charles Demuth, Arthur Dove, and Max Weber have turned up on Hull's walls in one form or another. In its changing monthly shows, the gallery most often features contemporaries, though the early works are always available for showing.

IFA IFA Galleries 2623 Connecticut Ave. NW 387-7537 Tuesday-Saturday: 9:30-5:30

After 30 years in business, Manuel and Bernice Baker continue to specialize in paintings, sculpture, and prints by contemporary Americans and Europeans, both representational and abstract. While framing constitutes an important part of the business, one-person shows change every three weeks, and have featured traditional realists like Tom Nicholas and Joseph Sheppard, abstract painters John Day and Joni Pienkowski, fantasy painter Joan Erbe, and sculptors Tony Padovano and

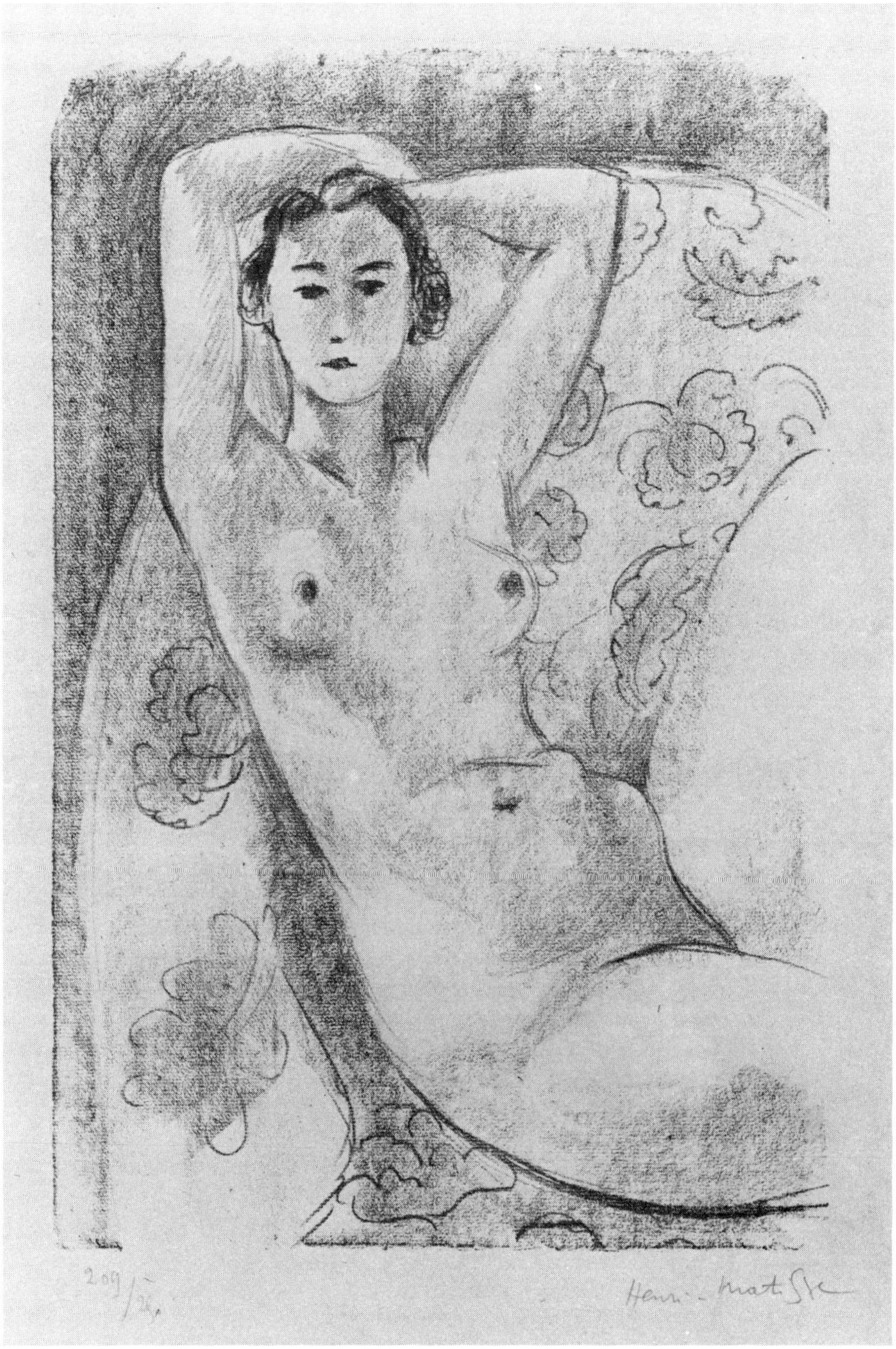

Club Copenhagen by Henri Matisse. 18¾'' x 12½'' lithograph. Hom Gallery.

Elliot Offner. Leonardo Nierman, Mexican painter and sculptor, also exhibits here.

The gallery stocks a large number of prints, by big-name artists like Picasso, Chagall, Agam, and Graciela Boulanger, along with work by Americans Harold Altman, Robert Burkert, and Bruno Zupan. There is parking behind the building, located across the street from Sander Gallery, which features contemporary photography. Both are near the Sheraton-Washington and Shoreham-Americana Hotels.

Intuitiveye Intuitiveye Gallery 641 Indiana Ave. NW 638-3232 Monday-Saturday: 11-5

This unprepossessing downtown gallery is located one flight up in a neighborhood on the verge of blossoming into a new downtown arts center. Specializing in contemporary photographers from all over the country, most of them budding professionals not yet widely known, the gallery often introduces several new talents at once, in theme shows such as "The Element of Mystery in Photography." All have passed the scrutiny of proprietor Sam Tamashiro, former photo editor for *National Geographic,* who is a well-known teacher.

Tamashiro also carries new and used books on photography and aesthetics and runs frequent—and popular—photo equipment exchanges from time to time. Prices are modest and discoveries can be made.

Local 1734 Local 1734 Art Collective 1734 Connecticut Ave. NW 797-9264 Monday-Saturday: 10-5

This energetic nonprofit collective of seven silkscreen artists banded together seven years ago to sustain both facilities for themselves and for a gallery to show work by lesser-known area artists. One flight up, a few blocks from Dupont Circle, the gallery occupies the front room, where well-publicized, open, juried shows change monthly, mostly involving original prints in various media including photography.

In the back is a silkscreen studio where fine graphics, posters, and T-shirts-to-order are printed. Reasonably priced silkscreens by gallery artists Laura Seldman, Ruth Stenstrom, Mari Foster, Jenifer Weiss, Julie Farrar, Nora Olgyay, and Sheri Lou Maeda are always on view in a bin, along with inexpensive works on paper by other local artists who have shown here. Each year the gallery produces a limited-edition silkscreen calendar with original prints suitable for framing. The "Edible Art" show in September is a popular annual event.

Lunn Lunn Gallery 406-7th St. NW 638-1300 Tuesday-Saturday: 10-6

Though Harry Lunn is known worldwide as a dealer in vintage photography and the work of Ansel Adams, he began as a specialist in the late-nineteenth and early twentieth-century prints by European and American masters. In 1971, the gallery acquired important graphics collections, along with work from the estates of Milton Avery and George

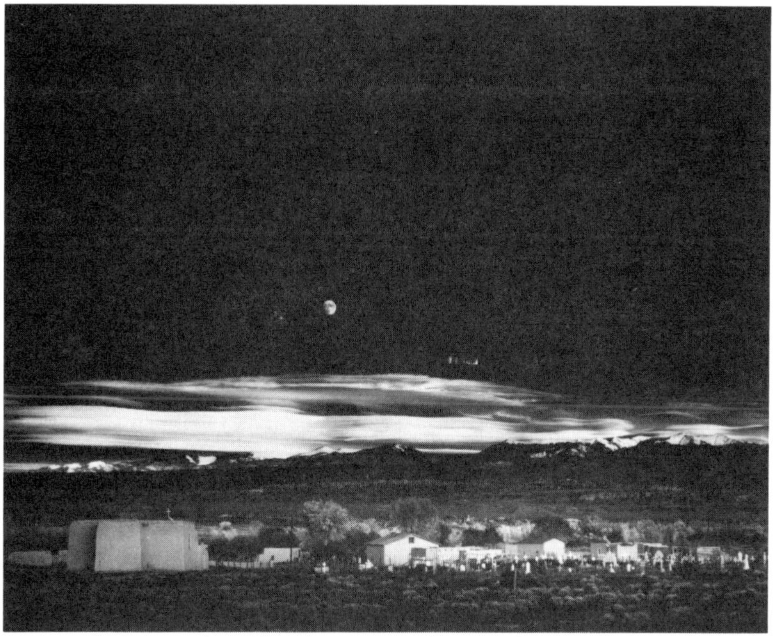

Moonrise, Hernandez, New Mexico by Ansel Adams. 16'' x 20'' photograph. Lunn Gallery/Graphics International Ltd.

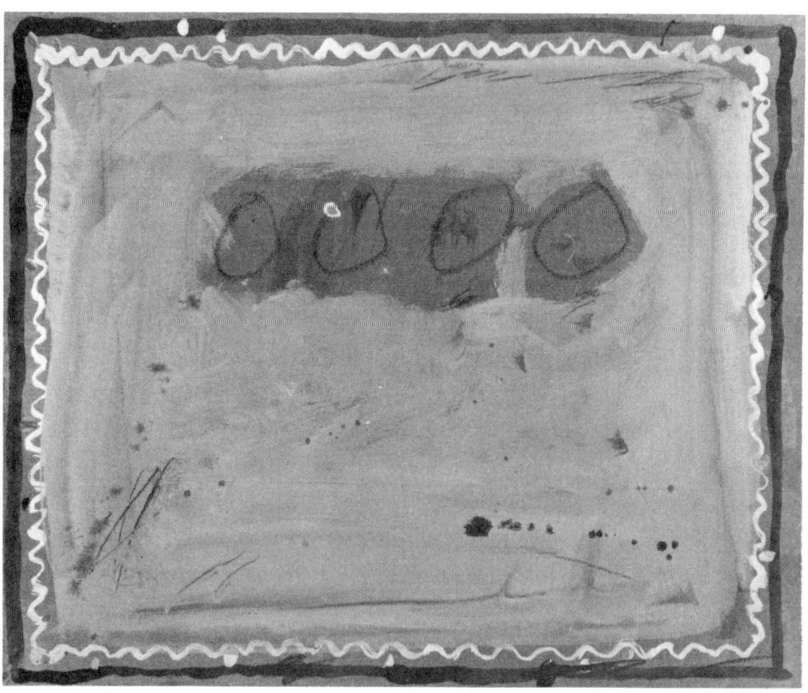

Four Circles 1979 by Gene Davis. 14'' x 11'' acrylic on canvas. McIntosh/Drysdale Gallery.

Grosz, and began to deal heavily at the wholesale level, which it still does.

But the extraordinary success of Lunn's first Ansel Adams show, also in 1971, led him to begin acquiring and exhibiting a broad range of important nineteenth- and twentieth-century photography. Since then the gallery's principal resources have been used to acquire significant collections of Adams as well as the archives of Walker Evans, Berenice Abbott, and Robert Frank. The gallery also owns vintage prints by early American, French, and English photographers Jackson, Watkins, and O'Sullivan, Fox-Talbot and Cameron, Bisson Frères, and Atget. Stieglitz and the Photo-Secession, as well as Lewis Hine and innumerable others are also well represented.

Lunn shows only a few contemporary artists, but does represent painter-printmaker Jacob Kainen and new talents Michael Clark, a neo-pointillist painter, and Kevin McDonald and John Grazier, both of whom make extraordinary drawings on paper. In the vastly expanded new space, Lunn expects to mount a larger and more varied exhibition program while maintaining the wholesale and museum sales which account for the largest share of the gallery's activity.

McIntosh/ Drysdale

McIntosh/Drysdale Gallery 406-7th St. NW 785-0872 Tuesday-Saturday: 11-5:30

Formerly Protetch-McIntosh (and before that Protetch Gallery), this establishment has been Washington headquarters for the more avant-garde art from all over the country for the past decade. The gallery founder, Max Protetch, opened a gallery in New York in 1976.

Since then his successor, former Cincinnati dealer Nancy McIntosh Drysdale, has broadened the scope of the gallery to include a varied group of painters, sculptors, and, occasionally, photographers, most of whom are working in the more advanced modes of contemporary art. The conceptual photographs of Peter Campus, sculpture by "Bum Shelter"-maker Jon Peterson, works by minimal evocateur Martin Puryear, "furniture" by Scott Burton, and installations by Alice Aycock and Patrick Ireland have been shown. Gallery painters include "New Imagists" Denise Green, Pinchas Cohen-Gan and Jon Borofsky, as well as pattern-painter Jerry Clapsaddle, famed stripe painter Gene Davis, abstract colorist Willem de Looper, and Ida Kohlmeyer.

Mickelson

Mickelson Gallery 707 G St. NW 628-1735 Monday-Friday: 9:30-5 Saturday: 9:30-4

Since the half-century-old Mickelson Frame Shop added a gallery in 1962, Sidney and Morris Mickelson have come forth with an extraordinary array of talent that always comes as a surprise, particularly after the trek through the disheveled-looking frame-shop area. They were the first dealers in America to show the prints of the late Dutch master-dazzler M. C. Escher, and his woodcuts and lithographs are still in stock. Mickelson also boasts a large collection of prints by George Bellows, Jack

Cox Recall, 1979, by Jerry Clapsaddle. 66½'' x 66¼'' acrylic on canvas. McIntosh/Drysdale Gallery.

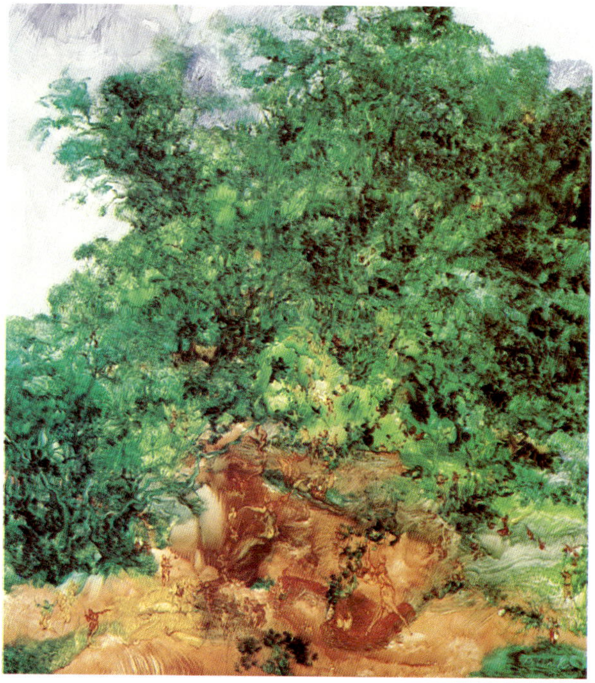

The Elements by Reginald Pollack. 48'' x 46'' oil on panel. Jack Rasmussen Gallery.

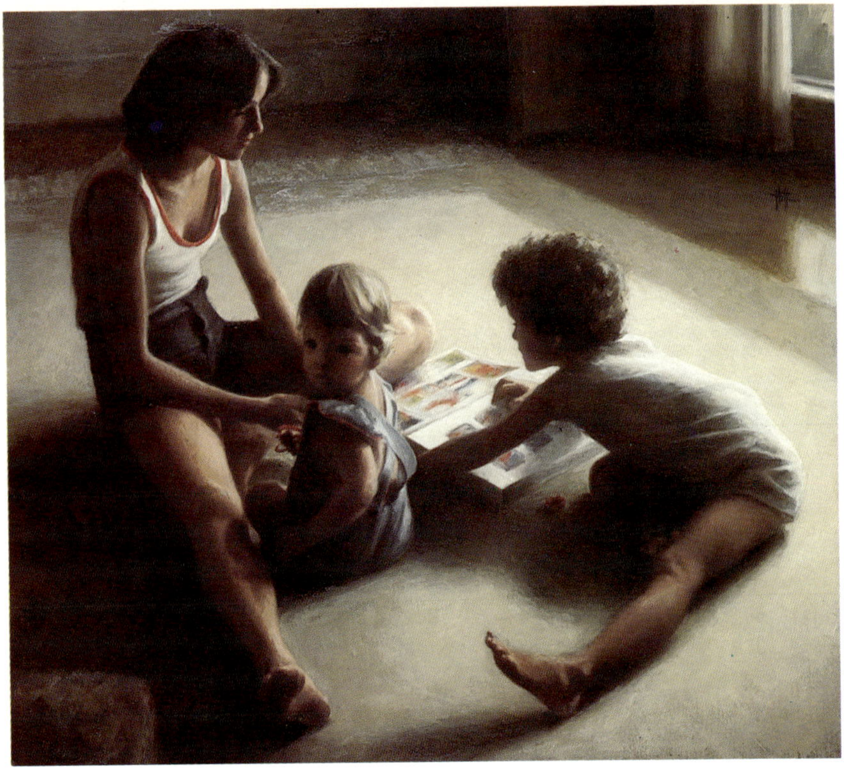

Playtime by Helen Hoffman. 21'' x 24'' oil on canvas. Veerhoff Galleries.

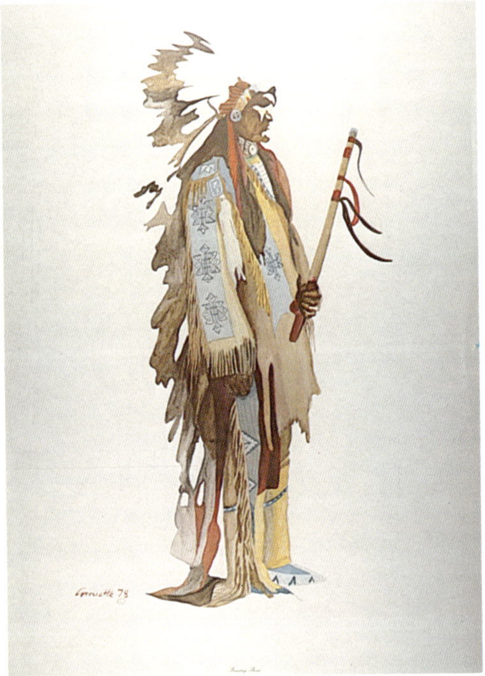

Standing Bear by Arthur Amiotte. 22'' x 33'' lithograph. Via Gambaro Gallery.

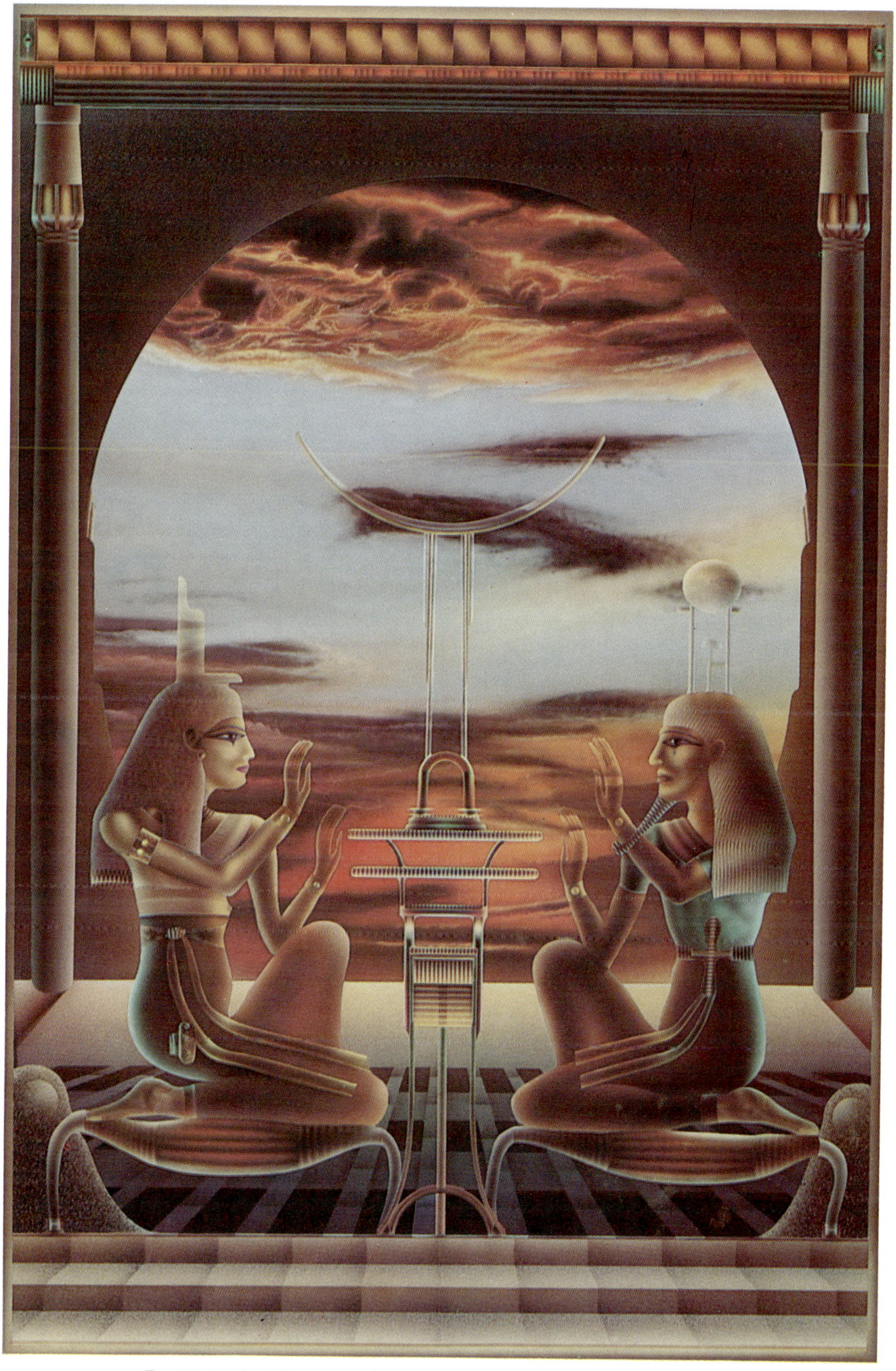

Ra Rising by Thoamas Akawie. Acrylic on board. Gallery K.

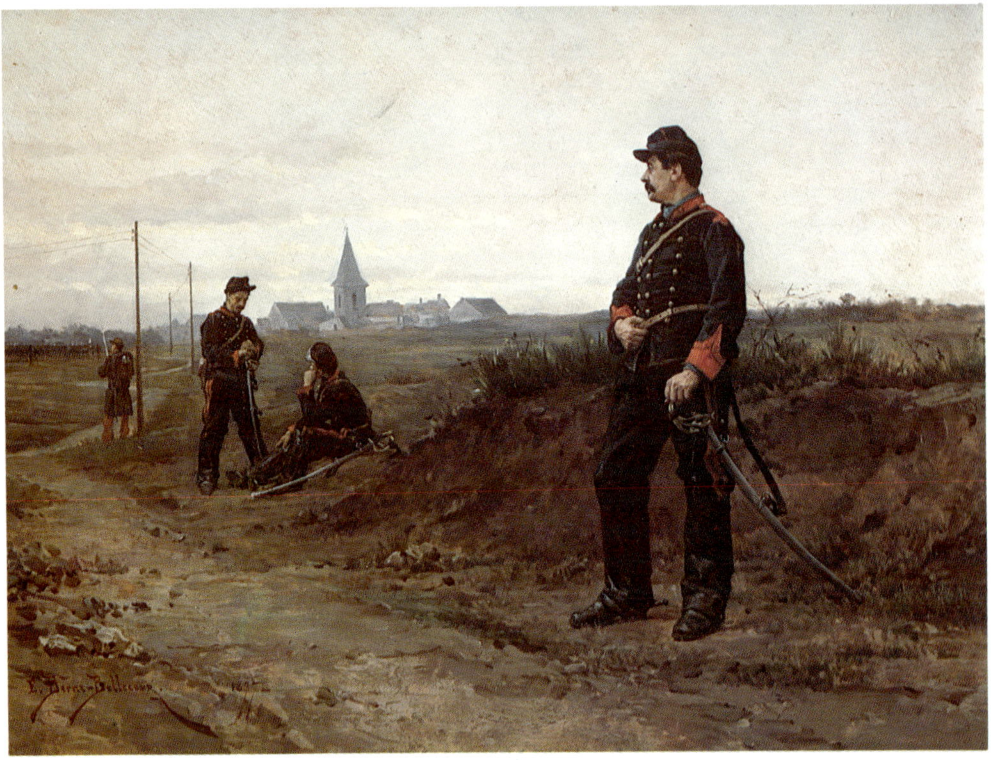

Soldiers Along the Roadside by Etienne Berne-Bellecour. 13'' x 18'' oil on panel. Pensler Galleries.

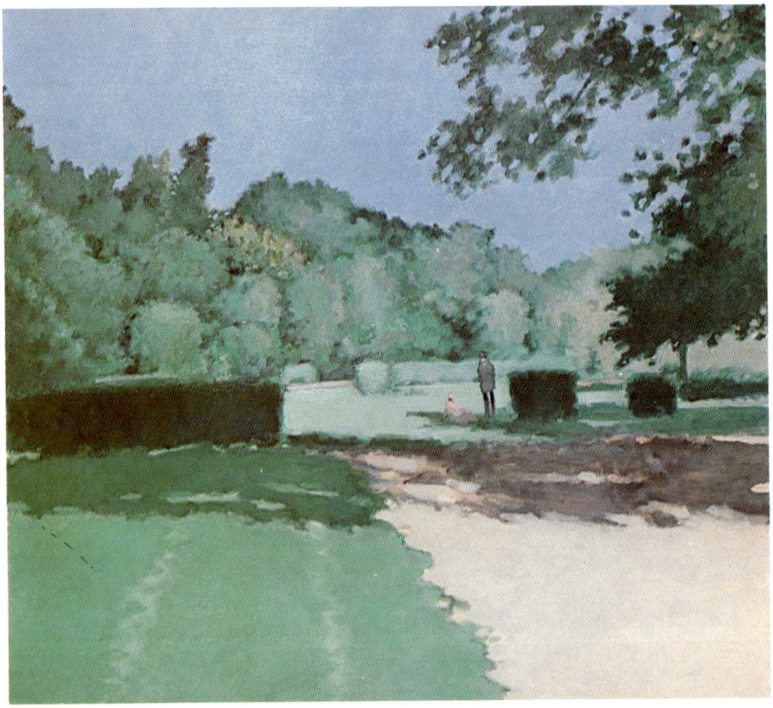

Touch of Autumn by F. McDuff. 36'' x 40'' oil on canvas. Venable Neslage Gallery.

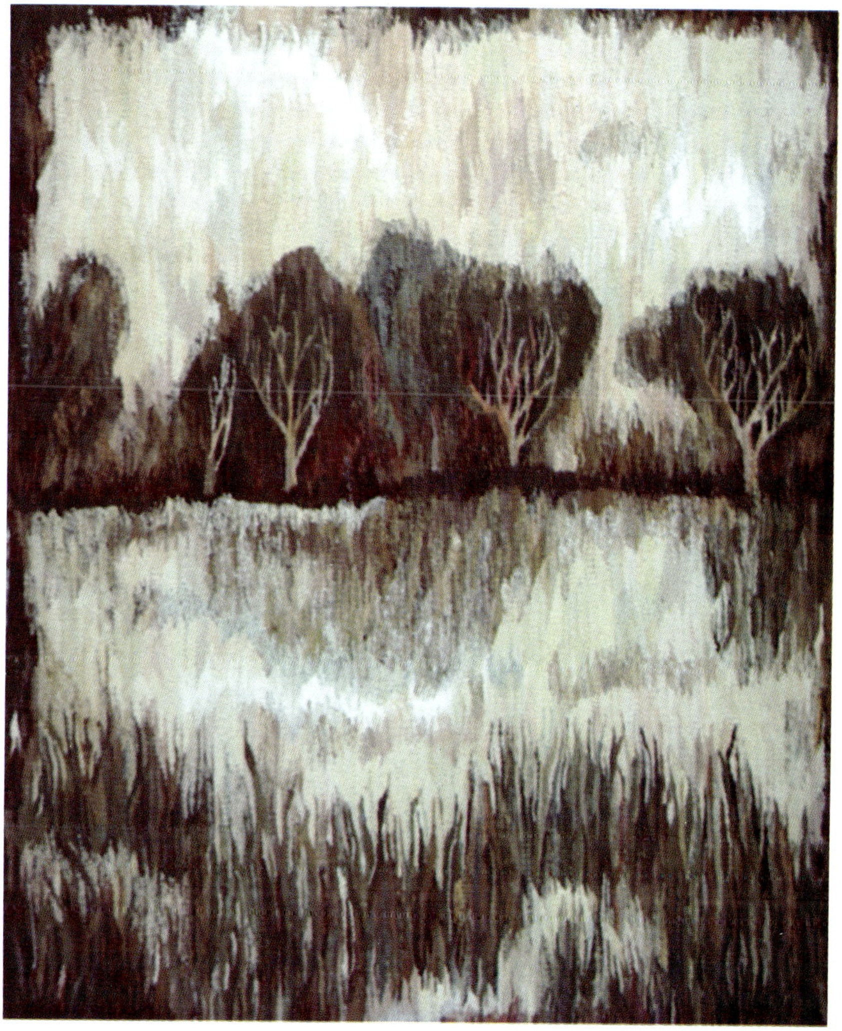

Naire by Ewa Szczerbic. 4'10'' x 5'8'' gobelin-tapestry. Old Warsaw Galleries.

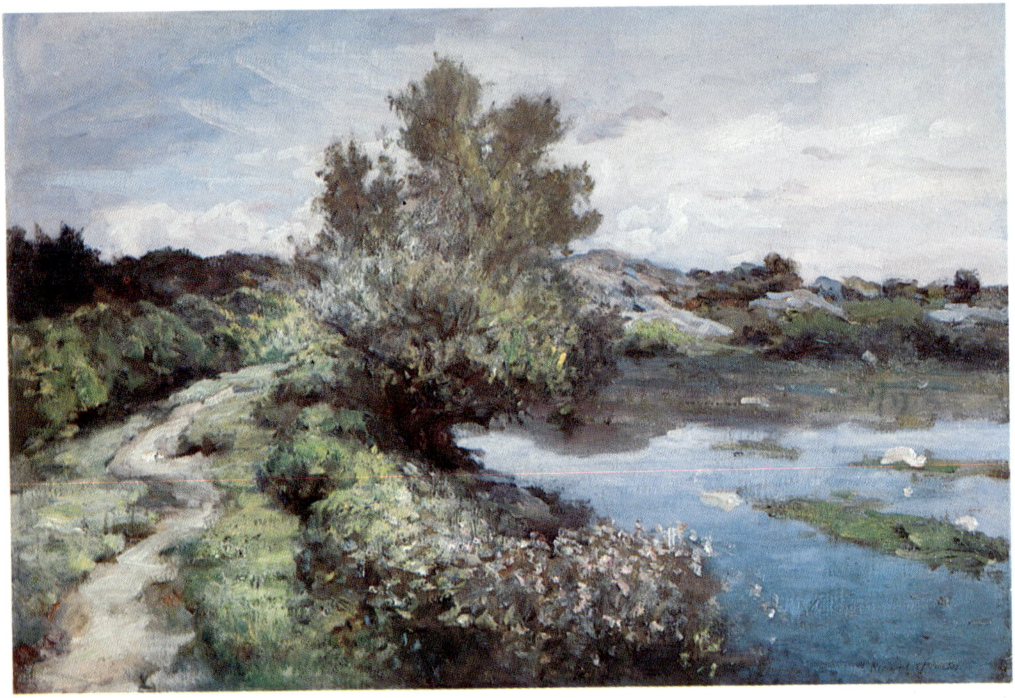

Maryland Countryside by Richard N. Brooke. 19½'' x 30''. Montrose Galleries.

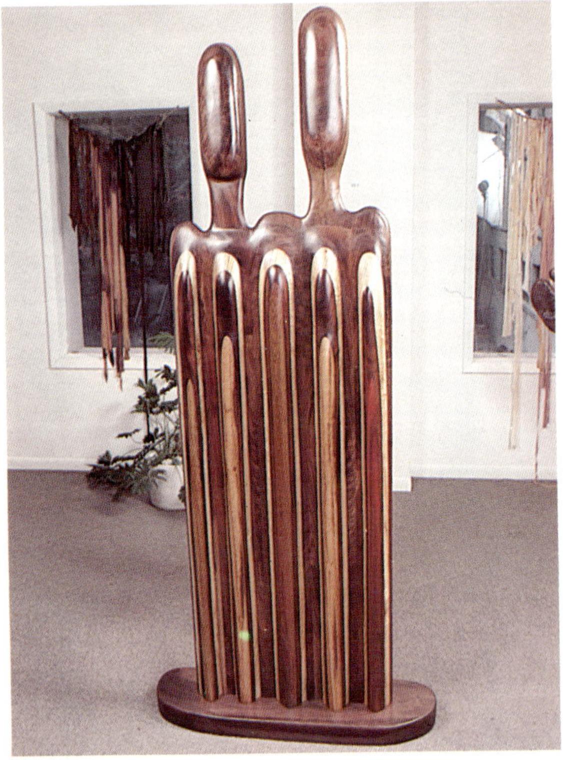

Majesty by Margery Eleme Goldberg. 7'6'' mixed woods. Zenith Gallery.

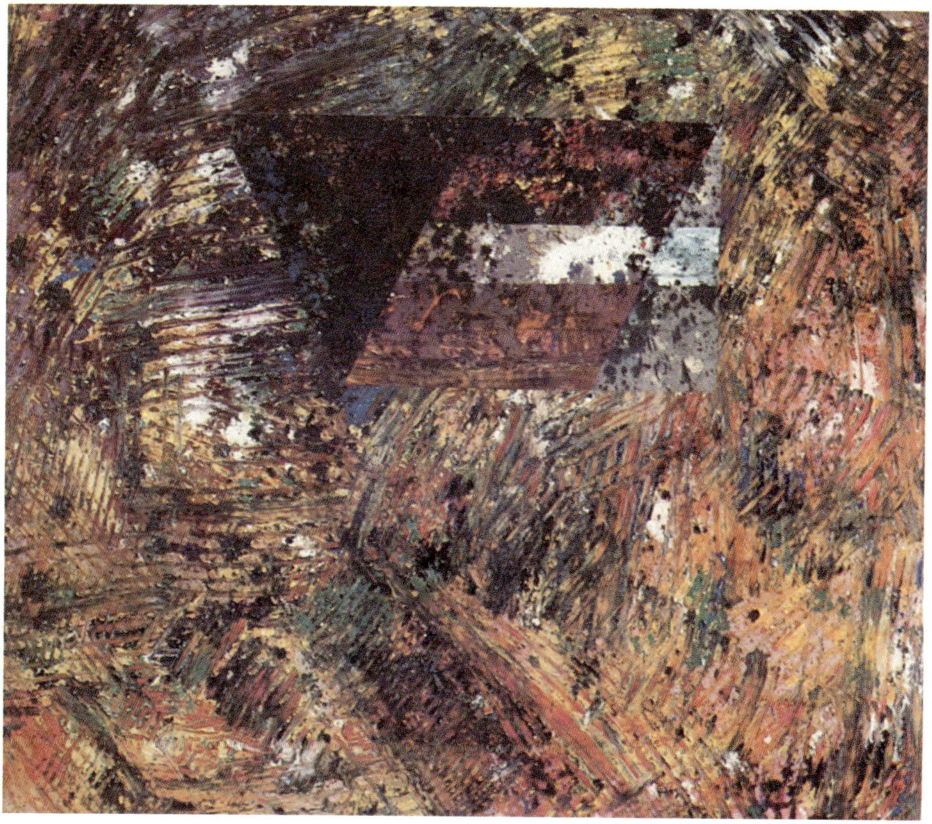

Evened Space by Sam Gilliam. 52'' x 68'' acrylic on canvas. Middendorf/Lane Gallery.

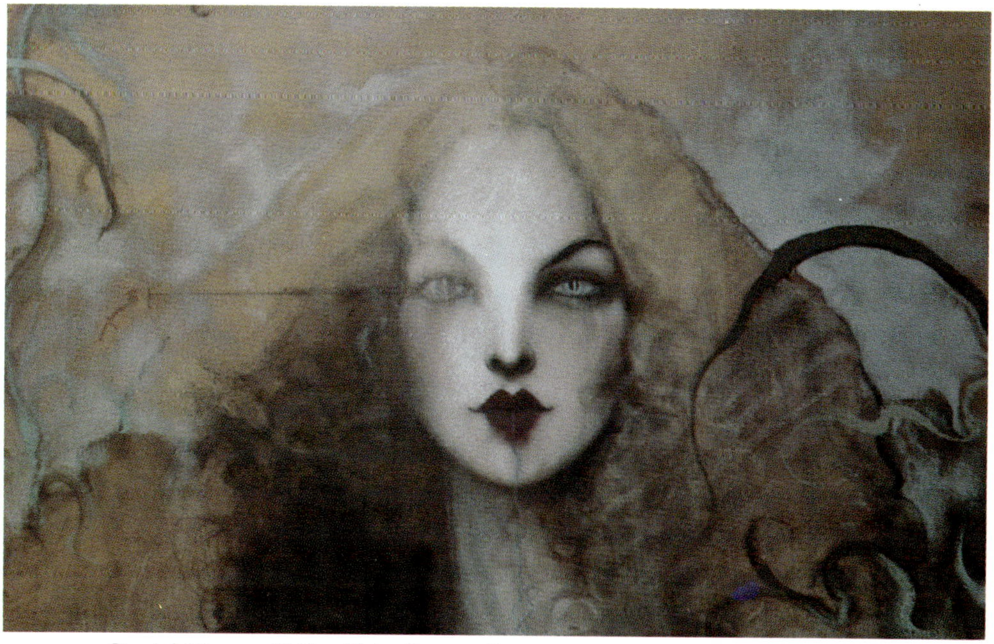

Special Women II (detail) by Ramón Santiago. 40'' x 50''. Zenith Gallery.

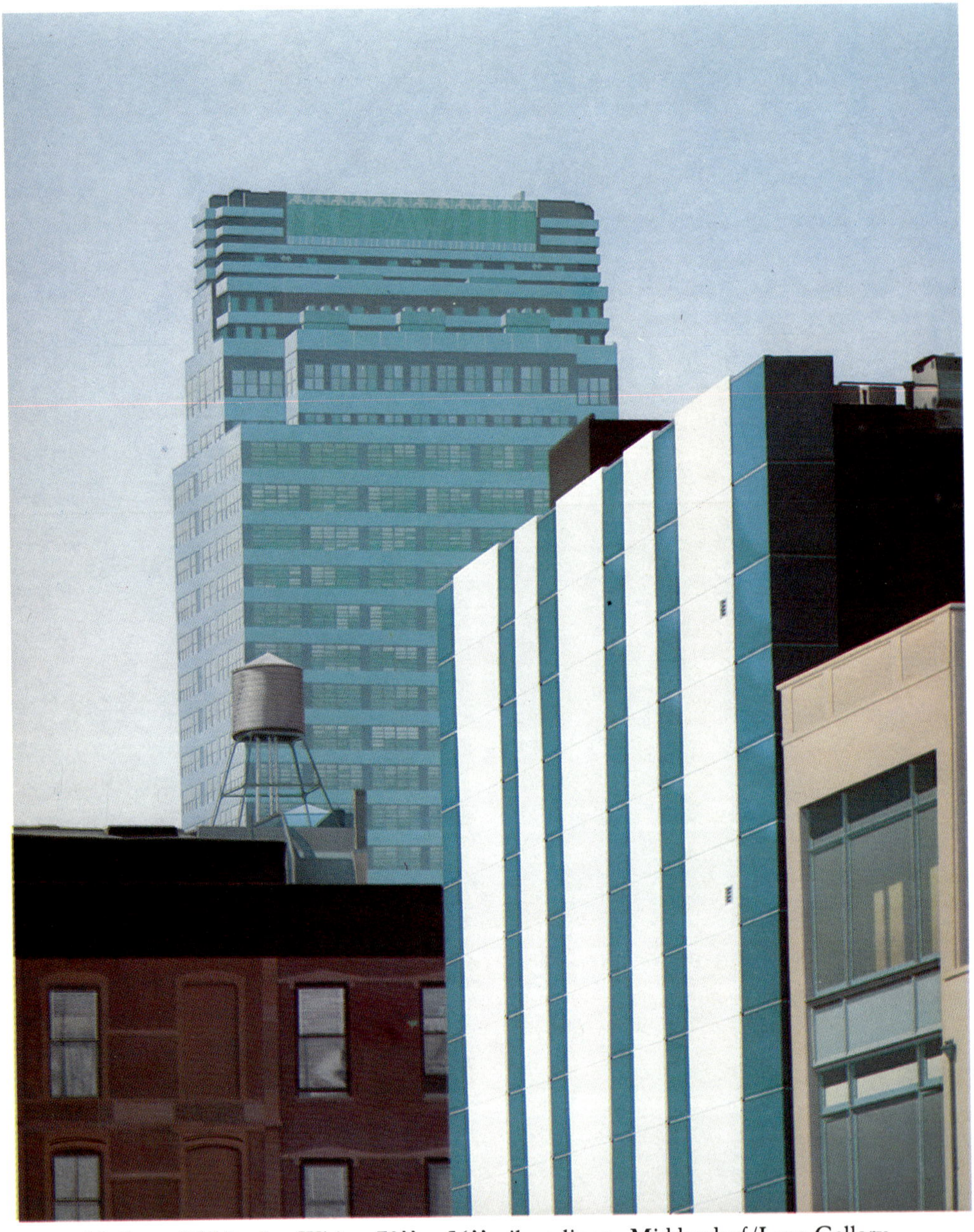

McGraw Hill by Joe White. 72'' x 56'' oil on linen. Middendorf/Lane Gallery.

Levine, Fairfield Porter, and Philip Pearlstein. The whimsical landscapes of English contemporary etcher Anthony Gross and mezzotints by Norman Ackroyd are also featured.

Mickelson's represents three important American sculptors who currently live and work in Rome—Milton Hebald, Peter Rockwell, and Robert Cook—as well as Dorothy Abbot who does Arp-like marble carvings. Summer group shows always include many leading contemporary American printmakers. The gallery is located just opposite the entrance of the National Collection of Fine Arts near the Gallery Place Metro stop.

Middendorf/ Lane

Middendorf-Lane Gallery 2009 Columbia Rd. NW 462-2009 Tuesday-Saturday: 11-6

One of Washington's handsomest new art spaces, Middendorf-Lane's two-story converted residence houses one of the city's best galleries for twentieth-century American art in all media. Owners Chris Middendorf and Palmer Lane support their interest in contemporary artists by dealing from their large stock of early-twentieth-century American prints by Stuart Davis, John Sloan, George Bellows, Childe Hassam, Martin Lewis, and Grant Wood, on up through contemporaries Richard Estes and Richard Diebenkorn.

Among the contemporary Americans, painters Alex Katz and Sam Gilliam and sculptors Ron Davis and Rockne Krebs have international reputations, while others represent top talent from Washington. Color painter Leon Berkowitz, minimalists Robin Rose and Jane Dow, realists Joe White and Joe Shannon, along with Tom Dineen, Stephen Ludlum, and sculptor Joe Ferrugia round out the group.

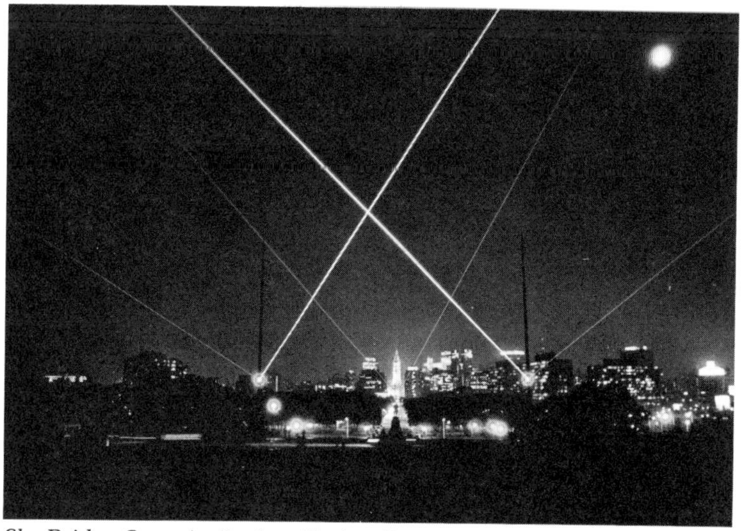

Sky Bridge Green by Rockne Krebs. City-scale laser light. Middendorf/ Lane Gallery.

Miya Miya Gallery 720-11th St. NW 347-6076 Monday-Saturday: 12-6

Since July 1976, this nonprofit, community-based educational gallery has devoted itself to showing the work of artists and craftsmen of African origin now living all over the world. The majority are from Washington, among them painters Ron Anderson and Al Smith, printmakers George Smith, Mary Greer, Malik Edwards, and Damballah Smith, sculptors Stanley White and Juliee Dickerson, and macrame artist Evélina Francis. The gallery founder and director is photographer and video artist Vernard Gray.

The gallery also publishes two newspapers: *Black Arts Review,* and *Kink: The Real Permanent,* which has to do with African hair-braiding techniques. MIYA has become headquarters for several braiding artists who provide this service.

In addition, poetry readings and musical performances are also held. "We have an open-door policy," says Gray, "and all artists are welcome to present portfolios." Appointments are advised. In fall of 1981, MIYA expects to move into the Lansburgh Building, 418-Seventh St. NW, with 26 other community-based arts organizations.

Montrose Montrose Galleries Suite 205, 7800 Wisconsin Ave., Bethesda, Md. 652-4199 Wednesday-Saturday: 12:30-5:30 and by appointment Closed August

American paintings of the nineteenth and twentieth centuries are the specialty here, with a sub-specialty in Washington painters who worked in this city early on and have only recently been rediscovered. Max Weyl, a turn-of-the-century German immigrant-watchmaker who made a fortune painting scenes of Rock Creek Park, is but one of many.

The gallery warns that paintings come and go quickly these days, but artists who have been in and out have included Bierstadt, Inness, marine-painter Frederick J. Waugh, Edwin Lord Weeks, George Hollingsworth, Harry Ives Thompson, and Chester Loomis.

The gallery has a conservator on staff who also offers private restoration services. Long-time collector Henry Glassie is the proprietor.

Old Print Old Print Gallery 1212-31st. St. NW 965-3777 Monday-Saturday: 10-6

Specializing in original eighteenth- and nineteenth-century American prints and maps, this decade-old Georgetown establishment is located just a few steps from busy M St. It has a very large stock which includes wood engravings by Winslow Homer and Thomas Nast, taken from old *Harper's Weekly* magazines, and prints from other publications such as *Judge* and *Puck*, which published political cartoons.

Of major interest are prints from George Catlin's 1841 "North American Indian Portfolio" and Carl Bodmer's aquatints made to accompany Prince Maximilian's journal, *Travels in the Interior of North America,* published in 1832-34.

Views of cities and landscapes taken from old books and newspapers

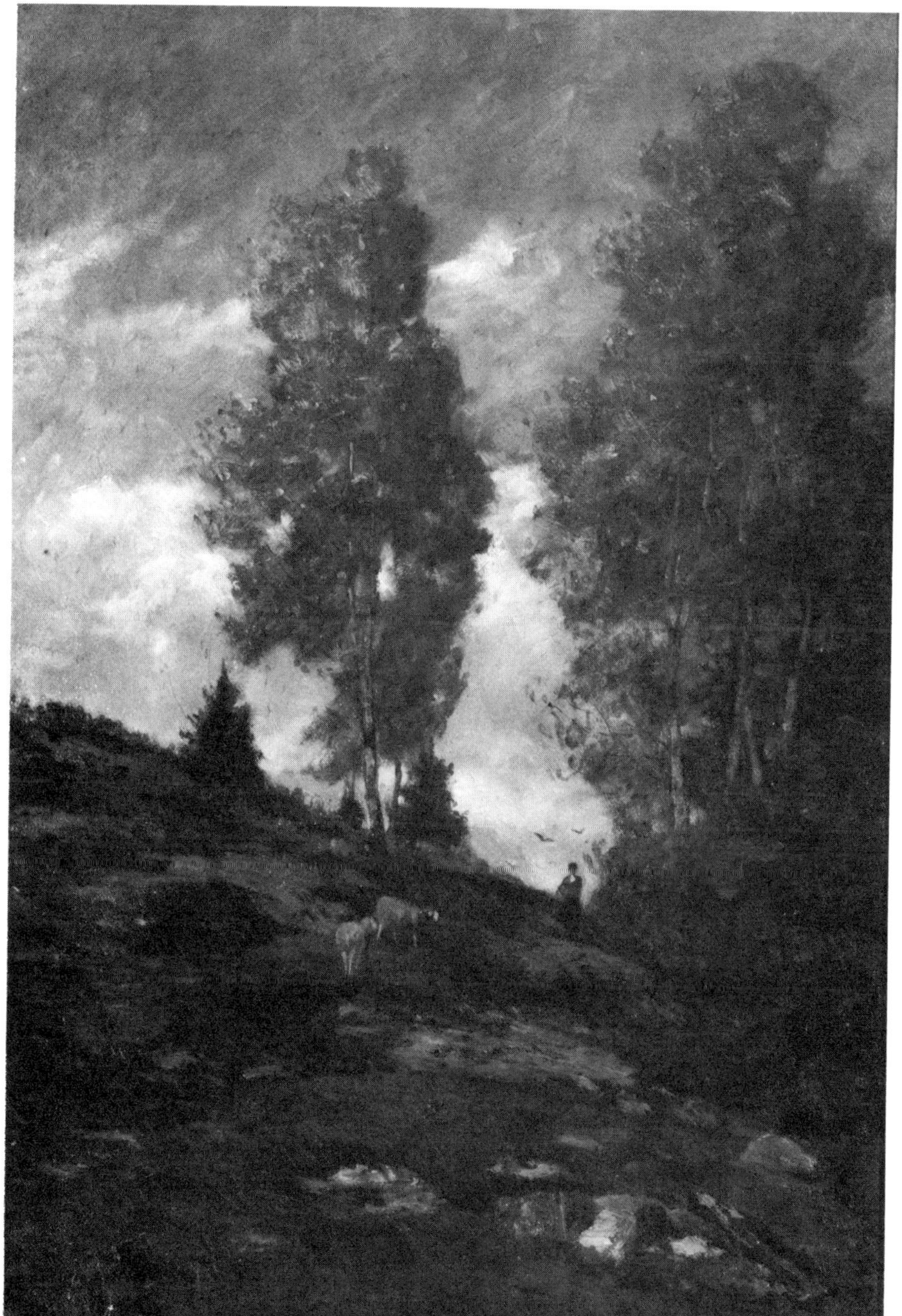

Untitled by Edmund Clarence Messer. 19½'' x 13¾'' oil on canvas. Montrose Galleries.
Galleries.

from all over the world are numerous, as are historical prints from the Civil War.

Natural history prints—flowers by Redoute from France and Robert Thornton from England, along with birds by America's Audubon—are also available. Proprietors are Judy and James Blakely.

Old Warsaw Old Warsaw Galleries, Inc. 319 Cameron St., Alexandria, Va. 548-9188 Tuesday-Saturday: 10-6 Sunday: 11-5

There is a fiery determination in the heart and mind of Barbara Witulska Lazo, Director of Old Warsaw Galleries, Inc. located in Old Town, Alexandria. This drive and purpose in her life is twofold: to promote Polish artists from all over the world and secondly to bring this art into American homes.

The gallery first opened its doors in 1975 and remains the only permanent art gallery in the area devoted exclusively to Polish artists both here and abroad.

A native of Krakow, Poland and long an art lover, Mrs. Lazo explains to visitors that in previous years, Polish artists were not able to gain recognition because of wars, changing governments, and lack of money causing many of them to migrate. Now, she believes the time has come to exhibit those artists whose work reflects the culture of their homeland.

Among the artists are John De Rosen, whose mosaics are included in the Vatican and major cathedrals of the world. Contemporary Polish graphic artists represented are Andrzej Pietsch; Jacek Gaj, Marta Kremer and Lesznek Rozga, Lucian Mianowski and Krystyna Marek-Swiecicka, an area artist, and a Corcoran Gallery of Art faculty member.

Andrezej Urbanowicz's oil paintings concern the existential while Henryk Fantazo's are surrealistic. Impressionistic painters include poetic imagination and the seriographs of Krystyna Marek-Swiecicka, a popular area artist, and a Corcoran Gallery of Art (D.C.) faculty member.

Andrezej Urbanowicz's oil paintings concern the existential while Henryk Fantazo's are surrealistic. Impressionistic painters include Ludwik Wiechecki in watercolors and Magdelena Spasowicz in oils. Sculptors include Andrzej Pitynski and Marion Owczarski. The latest addition to her collection is the famous Zygro (Zigmunt Grocholski).

Osuna Osuna Gallery 406-7th St. NW 296-1963 Tuesday-Saturday: 11-6

Osuna Gallery, formerly Pyramid, is now located in a renovated building downtown which it shares with several other leading dealers who moved from P St., among them Diane Brown, McIntosh/Drysdale, and Lunn. The basic interests of the gallery owner, Ramon Osuna, have not changed—paintings, drawings, and sculpture by a mix of contemporary American and Latin American artists, including Matta and Wilfredo Lam. The gallery has a special expertise in Pre-Columbian, Colonial, and contemporary Latin American art.

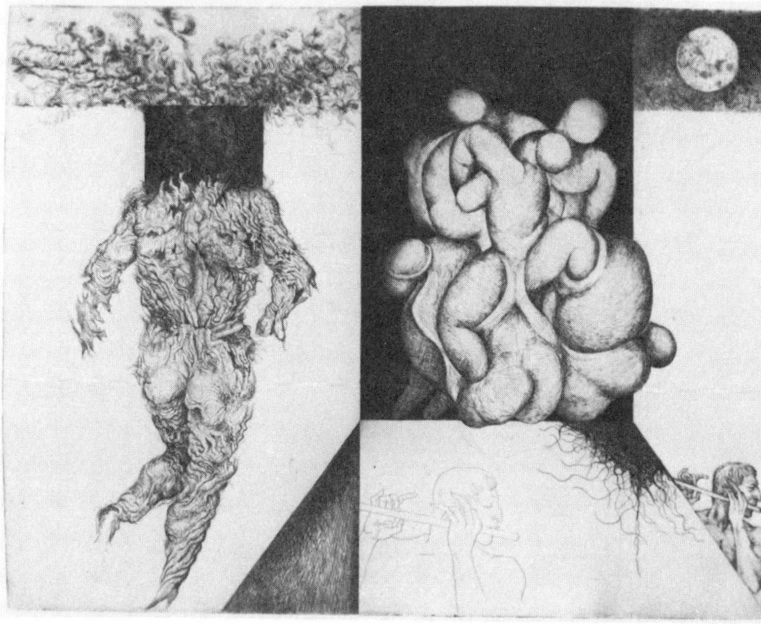

Penetration V by Leszek Rozga. 20½'' x 25½'' aquatint. Old Warsaw Galleries.

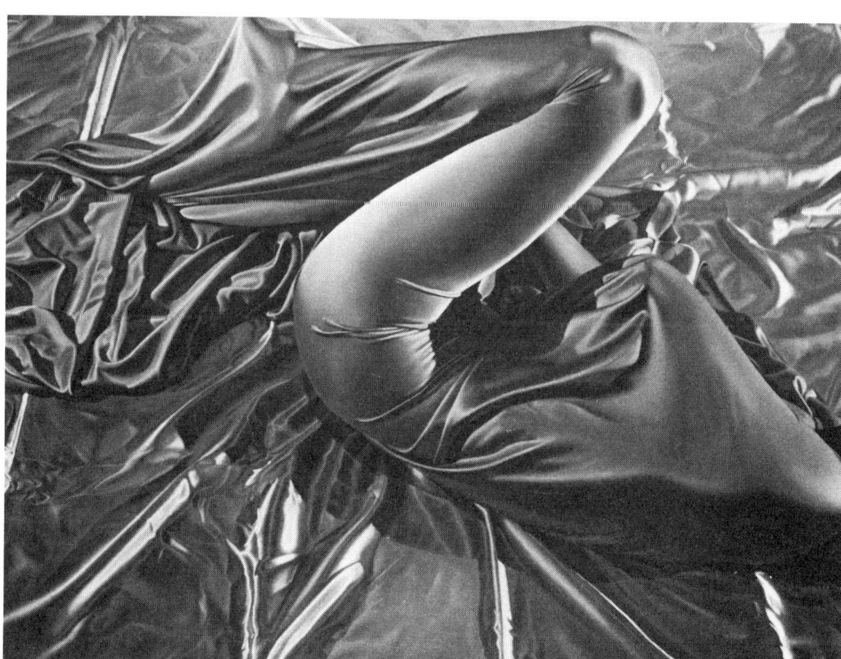

Sybarite by John Stewart. 48'' x 66'' acrylic on canvas. Osuna Gallery.

The majority of Osuna's changing monthly shows, however, feature contemporary North American painters and sculptors of various persuasions, from the minimal color painting of Tom Downing, the geometrics of Elaine Kurtz, and the sculpture of Ann Truitt to the realism of painters Rebecca Davenport, Manon Cleary, Stanley Sporny, and the work of acrylic sculptor Emily Benes. Abstraction is represented in the paintings of Phillip Wofford and the sculpture of Reuben Nakian and Jose Bermudez. Geny Dignac is a sculptor involved in more advanced, conceptual work.

Paul VI Paul VI Gallery 3720a Old Silver Hill Road, Silver Hill, Md. 347-1099 Tuesday-Saturday: 10-5

One of the area's most unusual galleries, Paul VI deals with art that has spiritual content, but not necessarily "church" art. "We try to avoid the pious," says Rev. Michael F. Farina, gallery director. The gallery is also ecumenical. The first show, in 1977, featured spiritual themes by Jewish artists Abraham Rattner, Leonard Baskin, Jack Levine, Ben Shahn, and Joseph Hirsch.

In their new location, just off Rte. 5 and Suitland Parkway (they were formerly located in Alexandria, Va.), the gallery continues to show a wide range of media from sculpture and prints by well-known artists like Rattner and Baskin to cloisonne by Sister Lucinda Hubing from Milwaukee, and canvases with cloth collage by Tatiana McKinney, whose *Resurrection* is in the Pope's private collection.

"We try to peddle our artists to the Vatican collections," admits Father Farina, who also occasionally arranges shows at the Apostolic Delegation. "We've also done well with the clergy, leading them to greener pastures," he adds. The gallery has arranged commissions for several of its artists in churches and other public places.

Other talent represented by the gallery, and exhibited in changing shows, includes figurative bronze sculptors Barry Johnson, Judith Brown, and Elizabeth Kormendy (one of the gallery founders); still-life painter Robert White, collagist Douglas Hendershot, printmaker Robert Enos, and young Peruvian-born painter Yoli.

"You can't ask people to make art with spiritual content and not offer them an outlet," explains Farina. The gallery is a project of the Institute for the Arts of the Archdiocese of Washington.

Pensler Pensler Galleries 1656-33rd St. NW 333-3565 Wednesday-Saturday: 10-5:30 Closed July and August

This tiny gallery, just off Wisconsin Ave. at the top of Georgetown, is for the collector interested in hunting down nineteenth-century American, and occasionally European, paintings, drawings, and watercolors. A private dealer since 1976, Alan Pensler opened this gallery space in 1979. His stock is small, but those who know the field will probably find something of interest.

Although the inventory changes, of course, one visit might reveal a late painting by Washington Allston, exhibited at the Boston Museum of

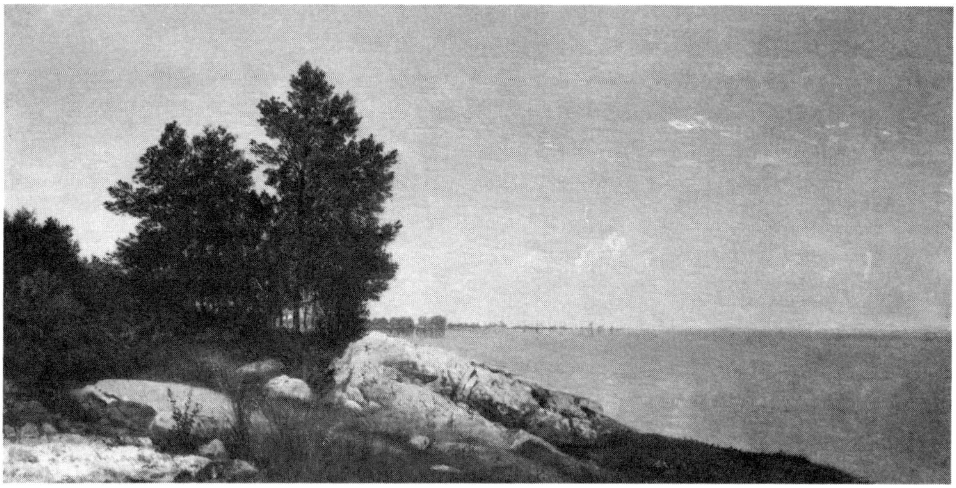

Long Island Sound at Darien by John F. Kensett. 15'' x 30'' oil on canvas. Pensler Galleries.

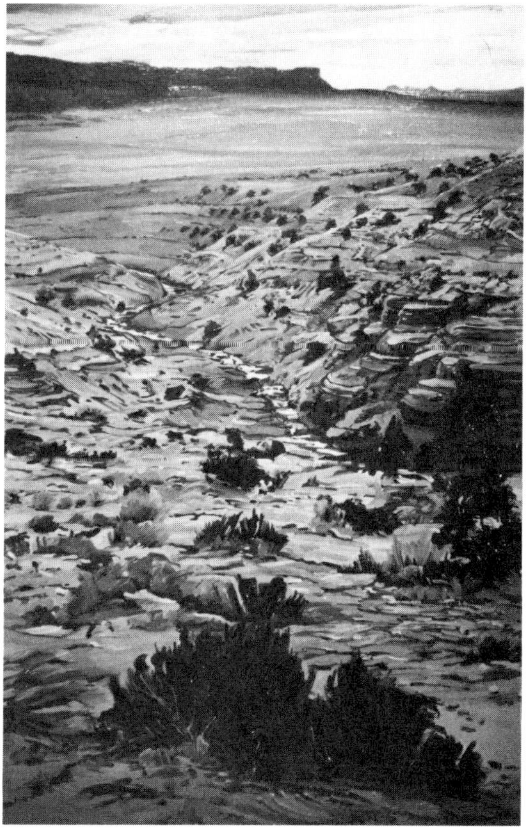

A Painted Desert by Stanley Sporny. 72'' x 48'' oil on canvas. Osuna Gallery.

Fine Arts in 1881; a luminist landscape by painter John F. Kensett, deaccessioned by the Metropolitan Museum in the late 1960s; drawings by American Impressionist Abbott Thayer and Maurice Prendergast, and a French genre scene showing resting soldiers by Etienne Berne-Bellecour, painted in 1877.

There are always portraits, still-life and landscape paintings by lesser-known nineteenth century painters, American, English, Italian, and French.

Plum Plum Gallery 3762 Howard Ave., Kensington, Md. 933-0222
Tuesday-Saturday: 11-4 Closed August

Located in what has become "antiques row" in suburban Kensington, Plum has proved to be one of the area's widest ranging galleries, and one of the top three in the suburbs. In their handsome quarters, the emphasis is on a broad selection of high-quality, upbeat art in all media and varied styles, from the handsome cast-paper sculptures of Hilda Thorpe to the tender fantasy unicorns of Jonathan Meader, one of Washington's most popular printmakers. Other area artists who've been given major exposure at Plum in monthly solo shows include master lithographer Tadeusz Lapinski, sculptor William Calfee, fiber artist Sirpa Yarmolinsky, and painters Frank Bunts, Luciano Penay, Alice Mavrogordato, and Patty Friend.

The gallery has also featured several artists from across the country, among them painter Sam Fischer from Houston and collograph-maker Walter Crump from Boston. Several craftsmen who exhibit in group shows include glassblower Dudley Giberson, ceramic sculptor Jeff Kirk, Rexford Brown, and Barbara Mones. An array of good prints by Stephanie Weber, Stephanie Evans, Carole Sue Lebbin, Stephan Minovich, and many more is always available.

The gallery is run by a highly knowledgeable group of Washington women who have also opened an in-town branch in the lobby of the jazz bistro, "Charlie's Georgetown," at 3223 K St. NW, where gallery artists will also be shown.

Premiere Premiere Galerie 7649 Old Georgetown Rd., Bethesda, Md. 951-0290
Tuesday-Wednesday: 12-6 Thursday-Saturday: 12-10

Formerly a co-op, and now privately owned, this suburban establishment is currently building a new stable of contemporary area artists. The range of media is wide.

Best known is sculptor, printmaker, and watercolorist Mildred Thompson, who has an international reputation. Painters Leo Saal, Joan Stoltz, and Natalia Klyova and sculptors Robert Charles Hudson and Kerry Witmer, who makes ceramic wall hangings, cover the stylistic gamut. Several printmakers are represented, among them Rosemary Feit Covey, Karen Gail Norman, and Janet Schnieder, who makes monoprints. Marguerite Richards combines printmaking and papermaking.

The gallery is located inside the Bethesda Square Shopping Mall.

Rasmussen Jack Rasmussen Gallery 313 G St. NW 789-2424 Tuesday-Saturday: 12-5

This brave downtown gallery, now three years old, has been championing several good area artists who have not had the recognition they deserve. As a result, the hard-working young proprietor, Jack Rasmussen, has successfully reintroduced the fantasies of virtuoso landscape artist Reginald Pollack, painters Robert Gates and Helen Herzbrun, and marble sculptor Sy Gresser.

Rasmussen, whose primary interest is in painterly painting; both figurative and abstract, has also exhibited a number of other area talents, among them Ed Zerne, Tom Green, Bill Dutterer, Dan Kuhne, Annie Gawlak, Laurie Kaplowitz, and Marianne LaRoche. Sculptors Walter Kravitz, who makes acetate paper installations, and David Staton have also shown here.

The gallery is located away from most other galleries, but just a few steps from the Judiciary Square Metro stop, F St. exit.

Rosen Paul Rosen Graphics, Ltd. 3417 M St. NW 333-6782 Tuesday-Saturday: 1-6 Thursdays till 9

Located not far from Key Bridge in Georgetown, this gallery deals chiefly in large-edition, commercially produced prints, usually published in editions of 100. American and European names are represented, among them the late native-American painter R. C. Gorman. Johnny Friedlander and Max Papart from Paris, Rene Carcan from Belgium, and Oku, a Japanese-American who works in a primitive style, are also on view. Bronze sculpture by realist Elizabeth Lyon and abstracts in marble, stone and wood by Harrison Steeves round out the selection.

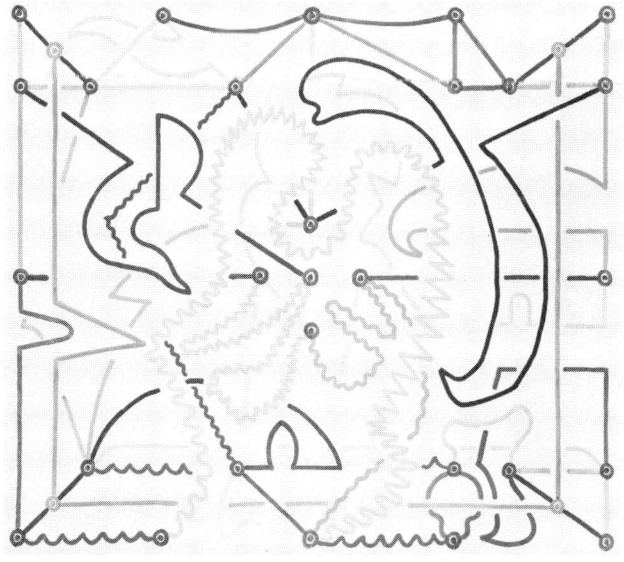

Ambush by Tom Green. 6' x 7' acrylic on canvas. Jack Rasmussen Gallery.

Sander Sander Gallery 2600 Connecticut Ave. NW 797-7307 Tuesday-Saturday: 12-6 Closed last two weeks in August

One of Washington's finest photography dealers, Gerd Sander specializes in work by contemporary Europeans and Americans, as well as in vintage material by August Sander, grandfather of the owner. Several other German masters, old and new, are represented here, among them Herbert List, Walter Peterhans, Wolf Von dem Bussche, Andre Gelpke, Heinrich Riebesehl, Floris Neususs, and Helmut and Gabriel Nothhelfer.

Sander also represents major photographer Lisette Model and two of her best-known students, Larry Fink and Rosalind Solomon. The great Josef Sudek, Lotte Jacobi, and Andre Kertesz, along with Washington color photographer William Christenberry, round out this high-quality stock.

Located one flight up in a pleasant new space (the entrance is on Calvert Street), Sander also sells some inexpensive vintage European work, along with a fine selection of books and catalogs on photography.

Seraph Seraph Gallery 1132-29th St. NW 337-5077 Monday-Saturday: 11-6

This Georgetown shop, opened in 1978, concentrates on contemporary American crafts and folk art, both utilitarian objects and purely decorative works. The range of media is wide, from art and production glass to fiberworks, silver jewelry, and candle snuffers, stained-glass panels and a variety of objects in wood. Contemporary Indian baskets and handmade quilts are also stocked.

What makes this shop unique, however, is the gallery space that adjoins it, where various media are explored—such as "Forms in Fiber"—and individual artist-craftsmen are featured in changing periodic shows.

Artists spotlighted thus far have included glass-blowers William Bernstein and James Harmon, and creative basket-maker Douglas Eric-Fuchs, who makes totem-like fantasy vessels from bark and twine. California basket-makers Fran Kraynek Prince and Neil Prince have also exhibited their highly unusual sculptural forms fashioned from palm fruiting blooms, torrey pine needles, and sea grass.

The gallery also features work in wood by Steve Madsen, who makes inlaid, carved walking sticks, and Rev. Herman Hayes, who whittles figures. Bob Trotman's "face-boxes" are featured.

Shogun Shogun Gallery 1083 Wisconsin Ave. NW 965-5454 Monday-Sunday: 11-6

One flight up over the busy intersection of Wisconsin Ave. and M St. in Georgetown is the Shogun Gallery, specializing in Japanese woodblock prints from the eighteenth century to the present day. Emphasis, however, is upon nineteenth-century Ukiyo-e prints and the so-called transitional period, from 1912-50, when woodblock prints were still very

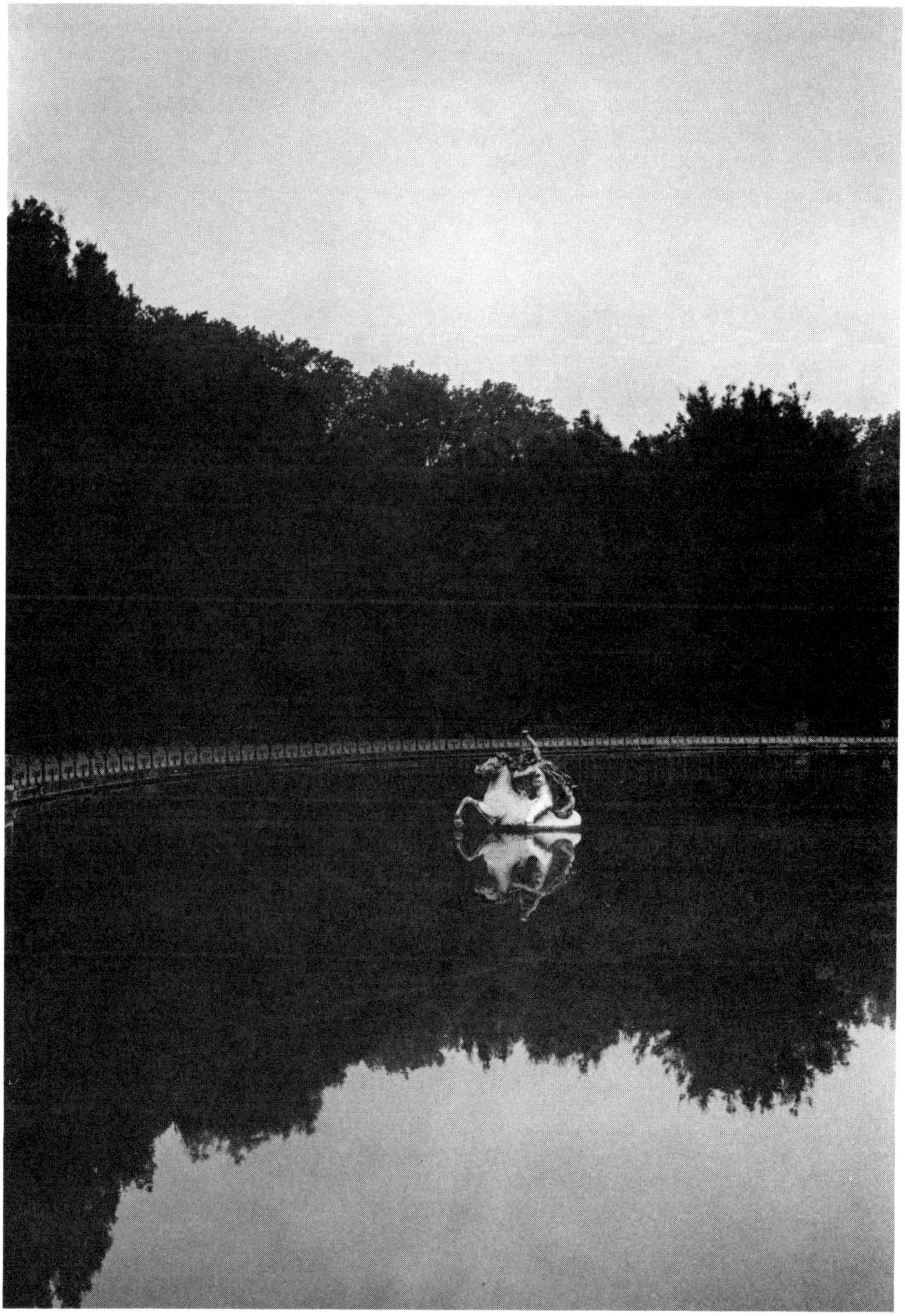

Florenz 1978 by Andre Gelpke. 8¾'' x 13'' photograph. Sander Gallery.

traditional in style, but had begun to incorporate Western perspective and modeling.

Among the better-known names represented in this large stock are the eighteenth-century master Utamaro, and the nineteenth-century Hokusai, Hiroshige and Yoshitoshi. Two of the finest landscape artists from the ''transitional'' period are Hiroshi Yoshida and Kawase Hasui, named a national living treasure by the Japanese government in 1956. Among the leading contemporary woodblock artists are Yoshitosha Mori, Jun'Ichiro Sekino, Toshi Yoshida, and many more.

The gallery owner, Toni Liberthson, is a longtime collector, and was a private dealer in New York before opening Shogun Gallery in 1978. Books on Japanese prints, as well as many posters, are also on sale. The gallery welcomes special-interest groups, and has broad knowledge of the merchandise it sells.

Spectrum

Spectrum 3033 M St. NW 333-0954 Tuesday-Saturday: 1-5 Friday evening: 7-10 Sunday: 2-5

This nonprofit artists' cooperative—one of the oldest in the city—shows a varied group of twenty-five area painters, sculptors, and printmakers who work in many modes, from abstraction to realism, and at various levels of accomplishment. The best-known painter in the group is Sandra Walker, who specializes in architectural themes.

One-person shows by members take place on a three-week rotating basis, with work by other members always on view. The gallery allows art to go out on three-day approval, with no obligation. New members are admitted by jury, and applications are welcome.

Studio

Studio Gallery 802 F St. NW 638-0515 Tuesday-Saturday: 11-4 Closed July and August

One of the city's best and longest-running co-ops, Studio is located just across from the entrance to the National Portrait Gallery, and is a worthwhile stop on any visit to this burgeoning downtown museum and gallery neighborhood. Studio is run jointly by 16 varied artists from Washington, most of whom also exhibit elsewhere in group exhibitions. Shows change monthly, giving each member a solo every two years.

Members change from year to year, but among the best-known of the core group are Val Lewton, a realist who paints city and suburban scenes; Pat Barron, who takes a hard look at politicians; Avis Fleming, who makes lyrical abstractions, and painters Rose Goding, Mary Louise Jecko, and John Morell. Linda Thern Smith and Ingrid Rehert are two good sculptors represented here, while Jon Eric Eaton of Baltimore is the sole photographer. Susan Foster, Caroline Huff, Sami Lais, Ralph Logan, Marjorie Hirano, and Tom Gilling also show here.

Studio occasionally sponsors community-oriented shows, notably large sculpture exhibitions which sprawl to the plaza outside. The nineteenth-century building that houses the gallery, incidentally, is occupied by several artists, dozens of whom have studios in this neighborhood. One

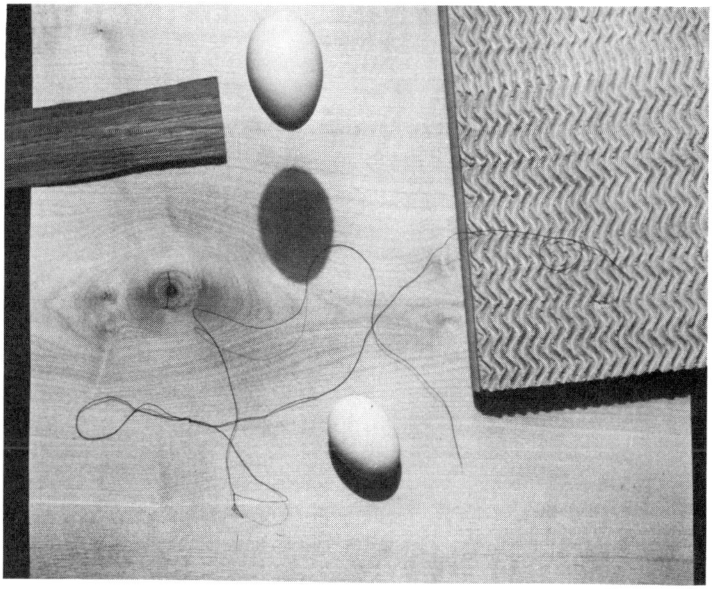

Untitled by Walter Peterhans. 8'' x 10'' photograph. Sander Gallery.

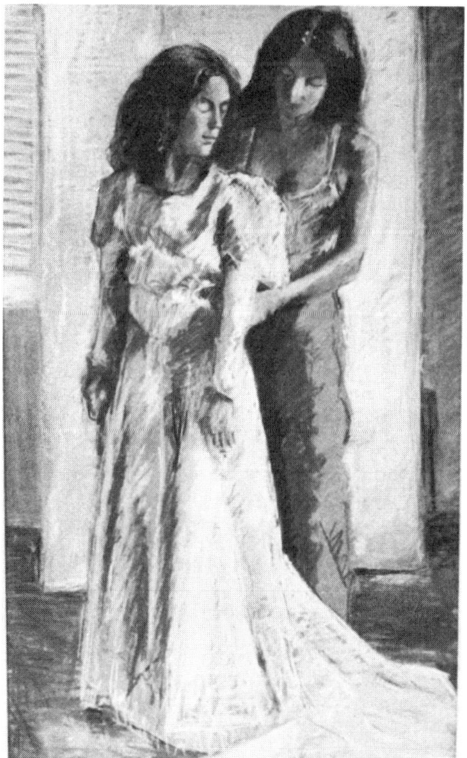

The Fitting by Jude Tolley. 24'' x 14'' oil on canvas. Tolley Fine Arts.

of the best is Frank Wright, who can sometimes be seen at work on a painting or print in his window just over the Donut Shop. (The chocolate-raised donuts are also highly recommended.)

Tolley Tolley Galleries 821-15th St. NW 347-0003 Monday-Friday: 10:30-5:30

''We opened this gallery in 1976 to have something pleasant to do,'' says lifelong collector Eleanor Tolley, whose husband, William, has been a calligrapher and framer in this location for years. The Tolleys' stock of nineteenth-century American paintings is small, ''but I've tried to buy things that are attractive, authentic, and that people will enjoy looking at day after day,'' says Mrs. Tolley.

''I won't buy just big names if it's a bad picture. I can vouch for everything in here, and it's all been authenticated.'' And she adds: ''I will not knowingly sell to dealers. I want to sell to someone who'll love the work. It's like selling kittens; how can you sell kittens to someone you don't think will enjoy them?''

The gallery's stock changes, of course, but visitors are most likely to find what Mrs. Tolley calls ''second-tier nineteenth-century Americans,'' including many landscapes by John Smillie of upper New York, Thomas B. Griffin, a painter of the Delaware Water Gap area, and James C. Nicoll, a marine painter of the northeast coast.

The Tolleys also handle some contemporary work, mostly traditional realists, including Anthony Watkins, a young landscape painter working in the nineteenth-century style; Lev Meshberg, a Russian dissident now living in New York; cowboy and Western bronze sculptor Truman Bolinger, and the Oregon animal and Eskimo sculptor Lorenzo Ghiglieri. Henry Woo, a well-known watercolorist from Mainland China, now living in the U.S., is also featured, along with V. B. Tankersley, who carves semi-abstract animals from semi-precious stones, such as crystal agate and pink and green alabaster.

Torpedo Torpedo Factory Art Center 101 N. Union St., Alexandria, Va. 836-8564 Tuesday-Sunday: 10-5

This gigantic art center, located on the Potomac River at the foot of King St. in Alexandria, was opened in 1974 in an old torpedo factory, thus the name. A Bicentennial project, the goal was to provide inexpensive studio space to area artists (under $4. per square foot) and, at the same time, to give the public an opportunity to see artists at work. More than 220 artists and craftspeople are currently working in the building on a daily basis. Visitors are welcome to prowl and buy directly from the artists. All work is done on the premises.

There are four nonprofit co-op galleries in the building. The Art League, a 700-member group of artists, runs the biggest gallery for paintings, sculpture, drawings, prints, and photographs. Each month a different area teacher or critic is invited to jury a show of work submitted by members, and it is hung in the gallery. All works are for sale.

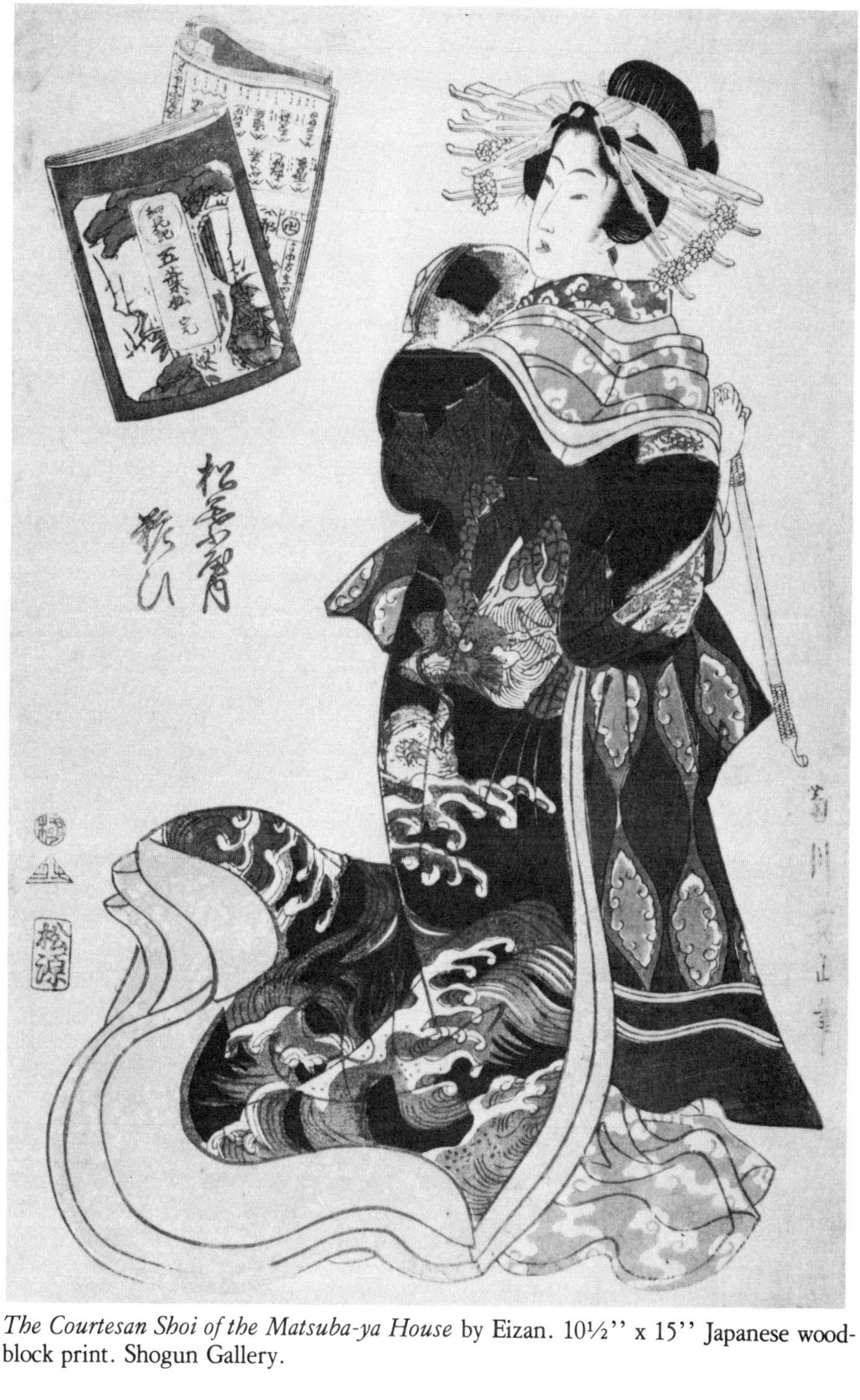

The Courtesan Shoi of the Matsuba-ya House by Eizan. 10½'' x 15'' Japanese wood-block print. Shogun Gallery.

Potomac Craftsmen, another shop on the ground floor, shows the work of 200 artists who work in fiber, and includes everything from woven shawls and skirts to baskets and batik.

Scope Gallery represents, in alternating monthly shows, ceramic work by the Ceramic Guild of Bethesda and the Washington Kiln Club.

Enamelists Gallery shows jewelry, wall-pieces, boxes, and other objects by 30 artists who do copper enameling and cloisonne. In addition, there are 17 workshops within the Torpedo Factory where other groups exhibit.

Touchstone

Touchstone Gallery 2130 P St. NW 223-6683 Tuesday-Saturday: 11-5 Sunday 12-5

There are 31 artist-owners in this co-op, and over-all quality has been climbing swiftly since the gallery opened in 1976. Work covers a wide range of media, from painting, sculpture, prints, ceramics, and photography to intriguing sculptures made from molded tapa-bark by Morella Belshe and quaint "portrait-benches" made from molded fiberglass by "Altina."

Wood-carver F. L. Wall makes unique sculptural furniture that imitates the ordinary objects around us: for example, a full-size, carved wood gasoline pump that opens up into a three-shelf cabinet, or a carved wooden fire extinguisher that could serve as a container for the real thing.

Several painters cover the gamut from realism to abstraction, among them Brenda Belfield (who was commissioned to design 44 stained-glass windows for the Washington Cathedral), Pat Fox, Chris Kidd, Ellen Liftin, Jo Harrop, Janet Wheeler, and Harriet Rosenbaum. Zinnia is the sole photographer, and Mansoora Hassan and Gretchen Friend-Jones combine graphics techniques with monoprinting. Judy Todd and Rima Schulkind are potters of far more than ordinary talent who produce both unique and production pieces in stoneware and porcelain. Todd also does architectural commissions.

The gallery features two member-artists at a time in shows that change every three weeks, work by each artist is always on view in the rear of the gallery.

Trocadero

Trocadero Arts of Asia 1608-20th St. NW 234-5656 Tuesday-Saturday: 10:30-7 Closed late August

More a shop than a gallery, Trocadero is included here because galleries featuring ancient art are a rare commodity in Washington. This two-year-old establishment, just a few steps from the Dupont Circle Metro stop, is apt to have in stock anything from an archaic jade bead to a Ming Dynasty painting. While they still deal in other antiquities, however, proprietors Kitty Higgins and David Kenny are now concentrating on bronze sculptures from China and the Himalayas dating from the fourteenth to the eighteenth centuries. There are also many modestly priced items on view, such as nineteenth-century bronze Thai Buddhas.

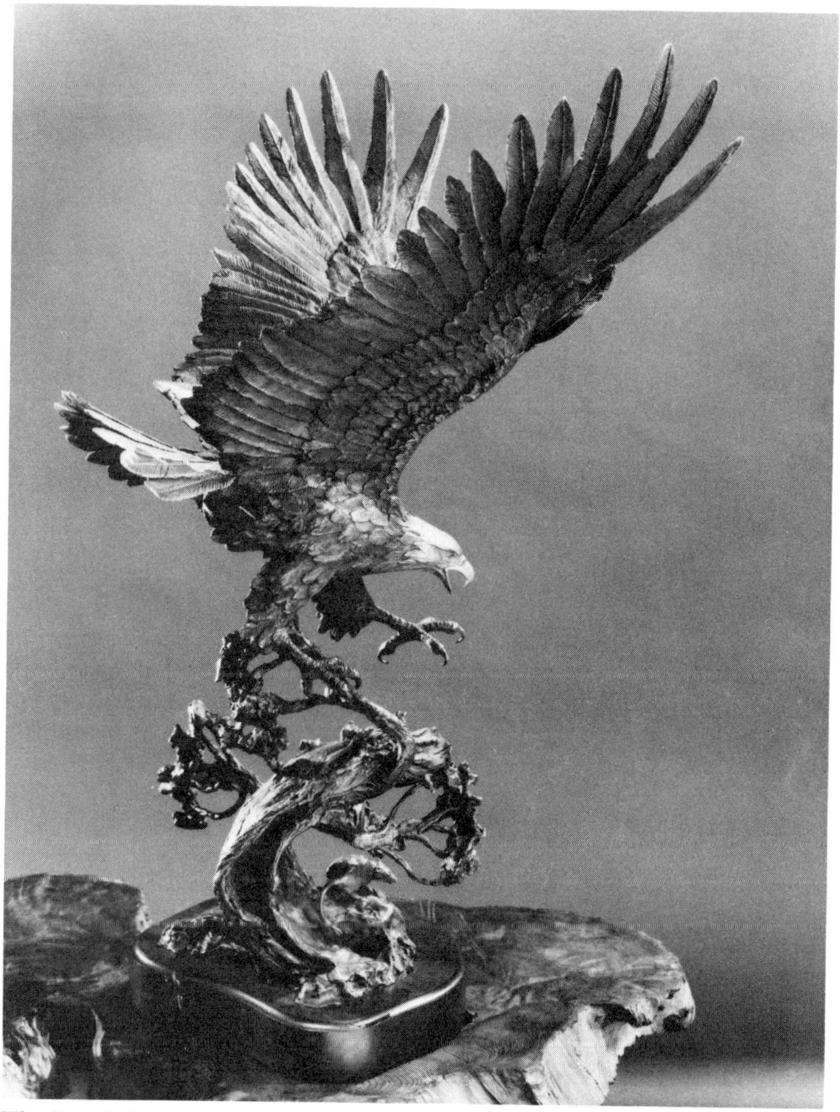

The Proud American by Lorenzo E. Ghiglieri. 27'' x 14'' bronze. Tolley Fine Arts.

Just down the hall is a room filled with Orientals, notably Turkish village rugs and camel bags.

Veerhoff

Veerhoff Galleries 1512 Connecticut Ave. NW 387-2322 Tuesday-Saturday: 9:30-6 Closed last two weeks in August

This traditional gallery, Washington's oldest, is run by Margaret Veerhoff, great-granddaughter of the furniture-maker, wallpaper-hanger and frame-maker who founded the shop in 1871. Framing is still a large component here, but landscapes, figure studies, and still-life paintings by contemporary American realists are exhibited in four shows each year, among them work by Helen Hoffman, Gladys Nelson Smith, and Molly Wise.

The gallery also carries a stock of eighteenth- and nineteenth-century European and American prints, a varied array that spans from Piranesi and Callot to Winslow Homer and Thomas Nast. There are many old prints of Washington, and others by Audubon filed under "Birds and Animals," and by Redoute and S. Curtis filed under "Flowers." There are old maps and a number of etchings and engravings by late-nineteenth-century Salon painters.

The gallery is located right on Dupont Circle, adjacent to Riggs Bank.

Venable-Neslage

Venable-Neslage Galleries 1742 Connecticut Ave. NW 462-1800 Monday-Saturday: 10-6

In operation since 1892, this gallery is still holding forth three blocks north of Dupont Circle. In addition to its framing business, it shows an assortment of work in various media by contemporary American and European artists, representational and abstract. Neo-Impressionist landscape painter Frederick McDuff from Washington, is a featured painter, along with two French artists, Marchelle Stoianovich and Souchie.

The gallery also handles prints by Miro, Calder, Gantner, Weisbuch, Secunda, and Michel Delacroix.

Via Gambaro

Via Gambaro Gallery 416-11th St. SE 547-8426 Tuesday-Saturday: 10-5 Sunday: 1-5

Devoted entirely to art by contemporary American Indians, this gallery was established in 1976 in a charming old carriage house on Capitol Hill. Visitors enter through a small enclosed garden which also houses the studio of gallery sculptor-founder Retha Walden Gambaro, who, with her husband, Stephen, has devoted herself to making the work of leading Indian artists of today better known. Many have never been shown on the East Coast before.

In the welcoming gallery space, one- or two-person shows change monthly, featuring work that is sometimes traditional, and sometimes highly advanced. Painting, sculpture, prints, and some extraordinary ceramics—some of them trompe l'oeil—are included in the gallery's busy schedule, along with group shows that spotlight new trends or

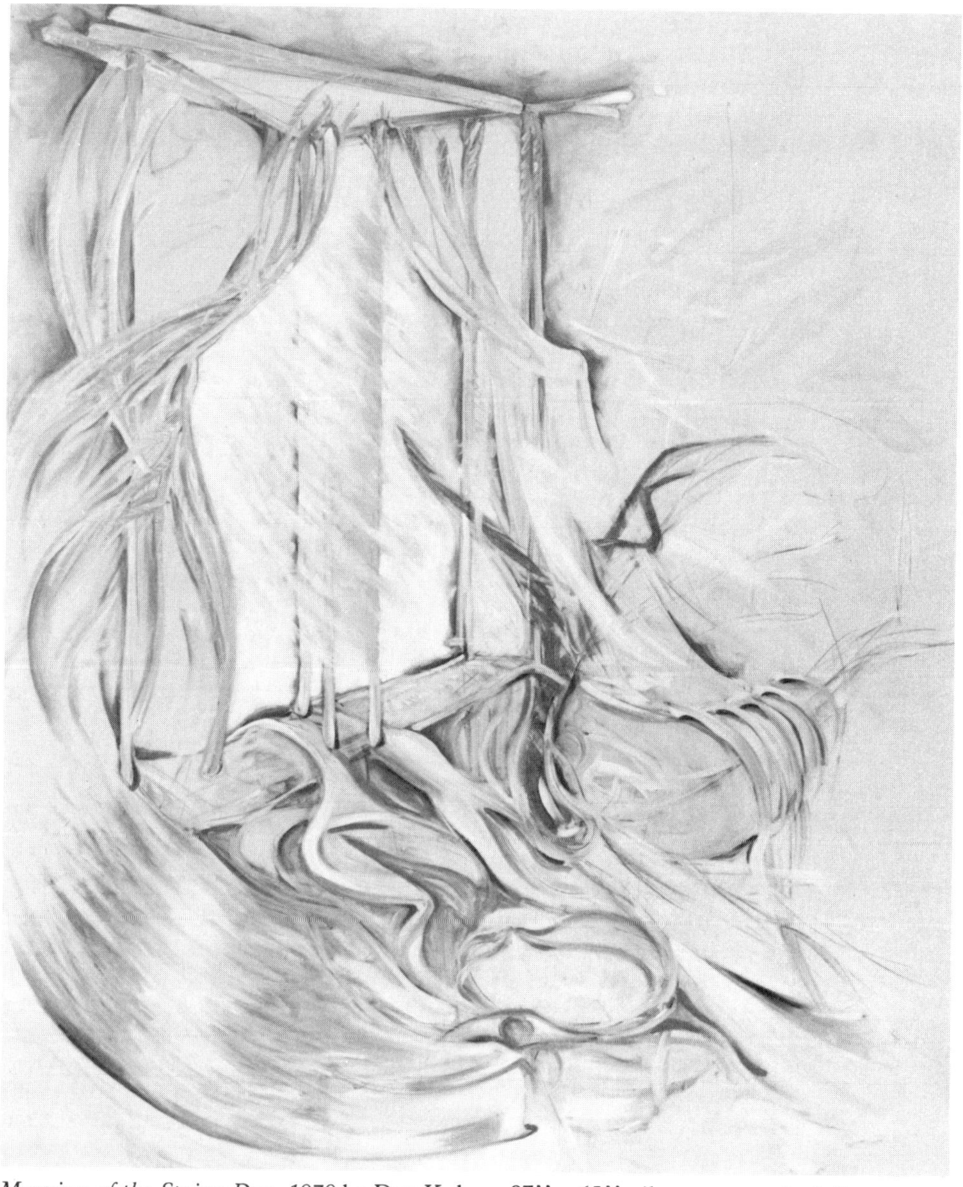

Morning of the Spring Day, 1979 by Dan Kuhne. 87'' x 65'' oil on canvas. Jack Rasmussen Gallery.

important new facets, such as "The National American Indian Women's Art Show" held in the summer of 1980. Kevin Red Star, a Crow Indian from Montana; Johnny Tiger, Jr., a Creek-Seminole; King Kuka, from the Black Feet tribe; Kevin Brown, Bert Seabourn, Val Jean Hessing, Helen Hardin, and ceramic sculptor Larry Des Jarlais are among gallery regulars.

The gallery is located three blocks from the Eastern Market Metro Station.

Volta

Volta Place Gallery 1531-33rd St. NW 333-9222 Tuesday-Friday: 12-6 Saturday: 11-6 Also by appointment

This small gallery, just off the beaten path in Georgetown, deals exclusively in quality traditional arts of Africa, with emphasis on ceremonial masks and statues. All works are used and "have some age," according to Mona and James Gavigan, the collectors who opened the gallery in 1980 after some years as private dealers.

The stock is small but select, and the gallery handles major works as well as less expensive objects for beginning collectors. Utilitarian and decorative objects, such as intricate beadwork, combs, jewelry, and fabric are also available. No African "airport art" will be found here.

Washington Women's Arts Center

Washington Women's Arts Center 1821 Q St. NW 332-2121 Tuesday-Friday: 11-6 Saturday and Sunday: 11-4

During its six-year history, WWAC has become a major force on the Washington art scene as an alternative space. Here hundreds of women artists (and a few men as well) have been given an opportunity to work, explore, and exhibit, some for the first time, others as part of soaring careers. Many of the painters, sculptors, graphic artists, photographers, and mixed-media artists have been catapulted into national prominence from shows at WWAC.

Supported by membership and grants, including several from the National Endowment for the Arts, this nonprofit gallery has been an increasingly impressive showcase in monthly juried shows, arranged by various groups within the Center membership, now 700 strong. An exhibitions committee oversees the program which usually includes annual group shows of printmakers, photographers, and multi-media. The Center's "Art World" seminar, which brings in dealers, curators, and critics to explain how the art business works, also produces one show a year. Curators from area museums, artists, and critics are often invited to jury shows, for example, "The Eye of Grace Hartigan," a sculpture show selected by Ann Truitt, and "New Faces," selected by a Corcoran curator.

The Center also runs an active workshop program, arranges poetry readings, and publishes a literary magazine annually. Exhibition catalogs are also published. Exchange shows with women's art centers in other cities, including Montreal's "Powerhouse," are among future plans.

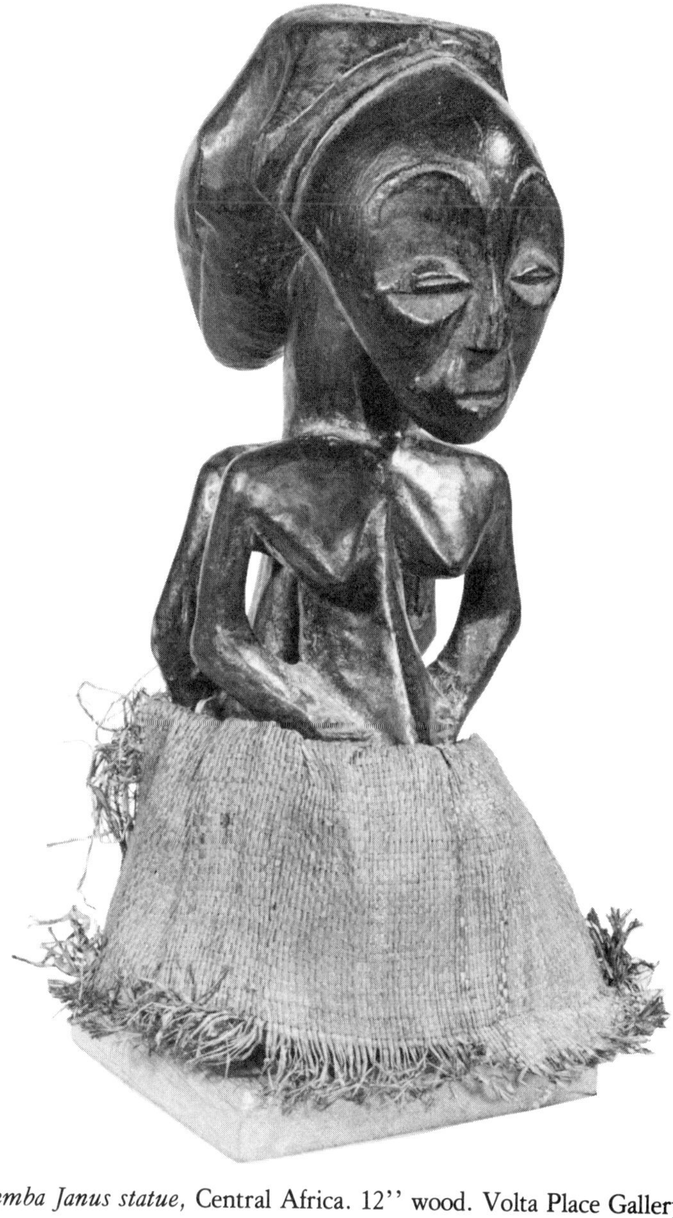

Hemba Janus statue, Central Africa. 12'' wood. Volta Place Gallery.

Washington World Washington World Gallery 3065 M St. NW 338-1275 Tuesday-Saturday: 10:30-5:30

This Georgetown establishment, one flight up over busy M Street, is the only gallery in Washington that sports a truly classy cafe, Cafe de Artistas. Here the food, like much of the art, is Latin American in flavor. The idea behind this combination was to foster multicultural understanding in every possible way, including an array of shows from all over the world filling the three floors of the two Victorian houses occupied by the gallery.

Since the gallery opened four years ago, it has cut back on the exhibit space somewhat, in response to the realities of the art market, if not to a reshifting of priorities. Exhibitions continue on the main floor, with a passing parade of contemporary art in every medium so democratically selected that quality seems sometimes to take a back seat. On the other hand, the stated purpose—"to give artists, particularly Latin American artists, a place to show"—is a worthy one, and shows of work by Benjamin Canas, a surrealist painter from El Salvador; Paez Vilari, a naive surrealist from Uruguay; and Washington artists Lydia Chamberlain and Peter Winant, have been worth looking out for.

The gallery is owned and operated by Jose Antonio Font of Cuba and Arnaldo Nannucci of Chile.

Woodfin Camp Woodfin Camp, Inc. 925½ F St. NW 638-5705 Monday-Friday: 10-5

This well-known New York photographic agency has now opened an office in downtown Washington to help deal more efficiently with the many professional free-lance photographers they represent in this city. A large number publish frequently under contract to the *National Geographic.*

The gallery—a large, pleasant room adjoining the office—was set up to exhibit the work of the photographers they represent, including Linda Bartlett's visual experiences of Ireland and a personal selection of images by James A. Sugar, who was chosen 1979 "Magazine Photographer of the Year," by the National Press Photographers Association.

Future shows will feature work by Thomas Höpker, Jonathan Blair, Sam Abell, and Karsh of Ottawa. Most of the work exhibited in these bimonthly shows is in color, with an emphasis on dye-transfer prints.

This building is also occupied by Ed Perlman and Inglett-Watson, designers and dealers in Art Deco furniture, objets, and prints.

WPA WPA (Washington Project for the Arts) 1227 G St. NW 347-8034 Tuesday-Saturday: 10-6

Since it was founded in 1975, WPA has become this city's leading alternative space, and the closest thing Washington has to a public window on the emerging art and artists of this city. It has also become headquarters-central for the thousands of artists who now live and work here.

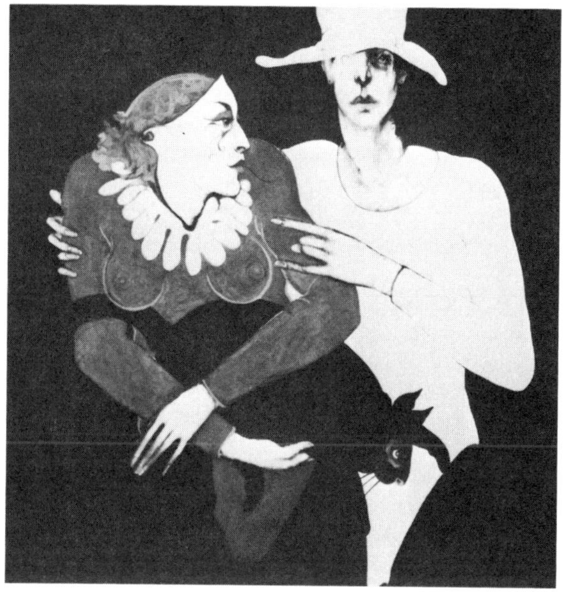

The Blue Cat by Ramón Santiago. 50'' x 54''. Zenith Gallery.

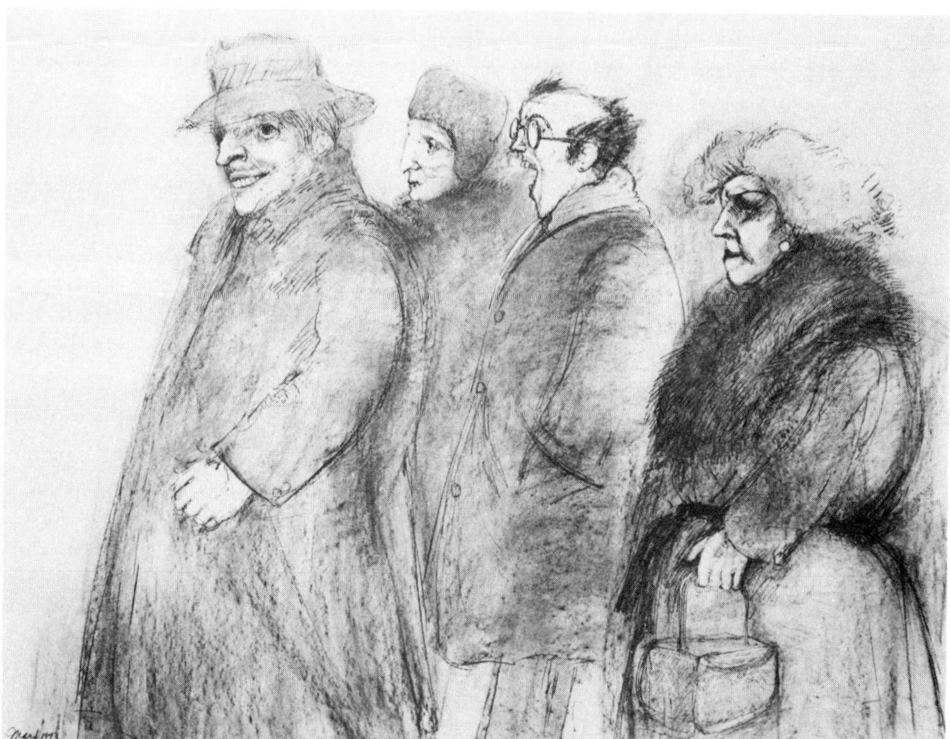

Winter Quartet by Marcia Marx. 48'' x 36'' charcoal on paper. Zenith Gallery.

Located in the heart of downtown, in a tidied-up three-story storefront building awaiting the wrecker's ball, WPA has survived on a shoestring of grants from the National Endowment for the Arts, the D.C. Commission for the Arts and Humanities, private foundations, and additional help from area businesses and individuals.

Despite this, it has become one of the best places in town to see not only new talent, but imaginative risk-taking exhibitions that explore new trends in all media, from a survey of area photography, organized by WPA's energetic director Al Nodal, to an examination of recent sculpture entitled "Stacking/Rigging/Binding: 10 Contemporary Sculptors," organized by Hirshhorn curator Howard Fox. Washington artist Terry Braunstein also served as guest curator for a revealing exhibition of artists' books called "Bookworks: Washington." WPA operates a superb little bookshop where unique, handmade, and small-edition artists' books can be purchased at very modest prices, including those of Braunstein and many more.

WPA has taken over two major outdoor sites—both nearby vacant lots—which it uses to commission site-sculpture by major artists from all over the country. Texan Bob Wade did the first installation, called "The Biggest Cowboy Boots in the World"; followed by Alice Aycock's "Game of Fliers" and "Overture: G-Strings" by Washington's Nade Haley, all at the corner of 12th and G Sts. NW Jim Sanborn was the first sculptor to do an installation on the newest site, a vest-pocket park at 1109 G St. NW.

WPA also has an active experimental dance, theater, and video program.

Zenith Zenith Gallery 1441 Rhode Island Ave. NW (rear) 667-3483 Monday-Saturday: 12-6

Located in a handsomely remodeled former carriage house not far from the corner of Massachusetts Ave. and 15th St. NW, Zenith Gallery is where the public can best see what's going on behind the scenes in this busy complex of artists' and craftsmen's studios. There are more than 50 studios located within the surrounding buildings; roughly half of the artists also live here.

The gallery often shows work by Zenithians, but not exclusively. In their monthly shows, paintings, sculpture, prints, and crafts by young American talent not given previous exposure in Washington is also exhibited.

A gallery regular is the energetic founder, Margery Goldberg, who makes superbly crafted, semi-abstract sculpture and unusual furniture carved from laminated wood of various hues. Painters who have shown here include Ramon Santiago from Rochester, N.Y., and James Carter and Andreas Nottebohn, both of whom work in airbrush techniques. Stephen Hansen from Michigan makes three-dimensional, comic-strip-like sculptures from papier-mache. Anne Maurice of Washington makes humorous ceramic animals posed as humans, e.g., "Foxy Lady."

James Ridlon, a professor at Syracuse University, the extraordinary Marcia Clay of San Francisco, and Suzanne Codi of Washington are other featured painters. ''Sica'' is a New York etcher who works on metallic paper; Ben Compton makes wearable art.

Other services available through the gallery include custom work in interior design, furniture, stained glass, ceramics, jewelry, ironwork, photography, video, and graphic design.

Artist Locater